Job Therapy

Job Therapy

FINDING WORK THAT WORKS FOR YOU

...

Tessa West

PORTFOLIO | PENGUIN

PORTFOLIO / PENGUIN
An imprint of Penguin Random House LLC
penguinrandomhouse.com

Most Portfolio books are available at a discount when purchased in quantity for sales promotions or corporate use. Special editions, which include personalized covers, excerpts, and corporate imprints, can be created when purchased in large quantities. For more information, please call (212) 572-2232 or e-mail specialmarkets@penguinrandomhouse.com. Your local bookstore can also assist with discounted bulk purchases using the Penguin Random House corporate Business-to-Business program. For assistance in locating a participating retailer, e-mail B2B@penguinrandomhouse.com.

ISBN 9780593714744 (hardcover)
ISBN 9780593714751 (ebook)

Printed in the United States of America
1st Printing

Book design by Alissa Rose Theodor

Some names and identifying characteristics have been changed to protect the privacy of the individuals involved.

I dedicate this book to my family—Jay, Matty, Jack, and Annie; my mom, Vicki; and my brother, Justin— who supported me while I wrote this book; to Quincey Pyatt, whose expertise was invaluable for bringing this book to life; and to my students, whose creativity and dedication inspire me daily, and whose research served as the foundation for most of the ideas in this book.

Contents

■ ■ ■

Opening | ix

1

THE CRISIS OF IDENTITY | 1

2

THE DRIFTED APART | 57

3

THE STRETCHED TOO THIN | 89

4

THE RUNNER-UP | 132

5

THE UNDERAPPRECIATED STAR | 178

Final Thoughts | 219

ACKNOWLEDGMENTS | 229

NOTES | 231

INDEX | 237

Opening

...

Most of us, at some point in our lives, will question whether we're on the right career path. For some, that questioning comes after months or even years of going to work in a state of low-level malaise. Nothing dramatic happened at work; there was no "oh shit" moment when you woke up in a cold sweat, realizing that you had made a catastrophic mistake by throwing yourself into a high-stress job like corporate law or running your own restaurant. But one day, you realize that you don't recognize the person you've become. The job has changed you, and not for the better.

For others, every day feels like a roller coaster; stressed and overwhelmed in one moment, calm and in control in the next. You're standing on a bed of quicksand, and small things, like a snide remark from your boss, are sufficient to make you question your commitment to your profession. But your job is stable, and it took you forever to get here, so you spend your time passively checking out job advertisements rather than actually applying for anything.

Our feelings about our careers are as rich and complex as the feelings we have about our relationships with our loved ones. We experience jealousy and resentment, ambivalence and excitement. Yet when it comes to making life-altering choices about these careers, often our feelings aren't what guide our decisions. Instead, the conversation about changing jobs, even among workplace experts, is usually centered around the structural and practical decisions we need to make. Do I want a job that is remote or one that is in person? Should I work for a start-up company that I believe in or take a stable (but boring) job at a well-established place? Most traditional career advice around job unhappiness and job change focuses on practical issues.

For *Job Therapy*, I decided to take a different approach and focus on people's feelings and their psychological relationship with their career.

As a psychology professor at New York University, I'm an expert on interpersonal relationships and communication. As a social scientist, I've studied the language people use in dozens of social contexts, from negotiations at work to interactions between physicians and patients in the doctor's office. Outside the lab, I've applied my expertise in the science of communication to help hundreds of people resolve conflicts in the workplace. My first book, *Jerks at Work*, applied tried-and-true techniques used in relationship therapy to tension-filled interactions between coworkers and bosses. When I started conducting surveys for this book, asking thousands of working people about their careers and interviewing people struggling with their careers, I noticed two striking things:

- People who were unhappy at work identified deeper psychological reasons for their unhappiness than the reasons we typically
  focus on: a lack of interest and burnout.

- The language people used to describe their feelings about work
  was similar to the language they used to describe their feelings
  about their relationship partners.

About two years ago, when we were all crawling out of the
pandemic, I noticed that the conversations I was having with people
about work were going in directions I hadn't experienced before.
I was talking with an employee who was accused of "taking over"
the work of her coworkers, when the conversation quickly turned
from a discussion about fraught relationship dynamics to a deeper
unresolved feeling of doing all of the right things to get ahead, but
still being passed up for promotions. I spoke to another person
who was dealing with a credit-stealing boss. We spent a few minutes answering the question "How can I protect my ideas?" before she told me, "I don't know if this career still defines me in the
way it used to." The people I spoke with would start with ostensibly solvable problems—or at least ones that felt constrained to
specific situations and relationships—but would quickly zoom
out, revealing big-picture problems and the deep psychological
struggles they were having with their careers. Something much
more was going on with people than bad bosses and salty coworkers, and I could sense it in the language they were using. They
weren't just talking about their relationships at work, they were
talking about their relationships with their entire careers.

I was curious if other workplace experts were observing the

same trend, so I checked in with Jacqui Brassey, coleader at the McKinsey Health Institute, researcher, and author. Jacqui has her finger on the pulse of workplace changes—and not just the structural ones we're seeing, but the psychological drivers behind them. She told me that although she, too, has noticed that many people seem unhappy with their jobs and careers, she has sensed that they are struggling to figure out why. There's an ambivalence in the air, she told me; people are torn between their desire for predictability, which is pulling them toward more traditional career paths, and their desire to break free from tradition. Throughout our conversation, she used phrases like a "big awakening" and an increase in "openness to new experiences" to describe these trends. Interestingly, our conversation was almost entirely about people's emotions and psychological states. We barely touched upon the structural issues that were dominating conversations among experts at the time, like changes in hybrid work.

▪ ▪ ▪

The other trend I identified was that the language people were using to describe their issues with their jobs and careers sounded a lot like the language they were using to describe their issues with their close relationship partners. Language can be subtle, but it's rich and full of clues about what people are truly grappling with. Statements like "I used to have a better handle on what my boyfriend was thinking and feeling, but now he feels like a black box" indicate a growing sense of psychological distance. Even indirect statements like "My doctor won't make eye contact

with me when I'm talking; instead, he stares at my chart" can reveal a deep-seated distrust of medical personnel. I've shown in
many contexts that the comments we make about our partners
can be even better predictors of our future behaviors than what
we say when asked what we plan to do. Language can give us a
wealth of information about people's states of mind, if you know
where to look. The use of language we usually associate with failing
romantic relationships—expressions of distrust and ambivalence,
for example—were common during my career conversations, which
made me realize a deeper shift was going on.

Therapy helps us manage all types of relationships. Why not
apply it to your relationship with your career? Therapy can work
wonders, especially when it's designed to help people not only understand what's driving their thoughts and behaviors, but also
develop the tools they need to open the lines of communication
between themselves and their potential new partners so they can
assess fit before diving into something headfirst. Just as therapy
can help people with their relationships with themselves and others, a therapeutic approach to careers can be transformational in
helping you figure out why you're unhappy at work so that you can
get closer to finding something more fulfilling.

We're all in a relationship with our career. And just like in any
relationship, we experience emotions that go up and down, and
that are often the result of deep psychological issues we don't always understand. *Job Therapy* was born out of the idea that unpacking these psychological issues is the first and arguably most
important step in discovering happiness at work. It's a new approach to career navigation designed to help you learn new things

about yourself and learn new strategies of communication so you leave little of your future career happiness up to chance.

To understand career goers, I studied them in a way they haven't been studied before. There are hundreds of studies on the modern career goer (people who are questioning their happiness at work and starting to analyze new opportunities)—what they want out of a job, what they're willing to tolerate, how many want to switch careers entirely. The workplace has changed a lot in the last several years, and experts are quick to document how people are adapting to shifting tides.

But as I've mentioned, this work doesn't really get at the deep underpinnings of our unhappiness at work. At best, it scratches the surface with concepts like burnout and work-life balance. The questions I had were broader and more psychologically basic: What leads us to de-identify with something we spent decades pursuing? How often and why do we sabotage our own progress at work, volunteering to do things we don't have the time or mental energy for? How much of our inability to get that raise and promotion is about our own shortcomings, like misreading our status at work, and how much is it due to the shortcomings of those around us, like a boss who doesn't have enough status to influence promotion decisions?

To get at answers to these questions, I needed to first take a step back to evaluate what makes a person begin questioning their relationship with their career. In the study of close relationships, there's been a lot of research on the risk factors of divorce, including precipitating events that kick-start the process of contemplating exit. Structural events, like sudden changes in income and having children, and psychological concerns, like an unfair allocation of household labor, which can lead people to feel underappreciated and invisible, are critical opportunities for intervention through therapy. If you can capture people at these times, you have a good chance not only of helping them process what's happening in the relationship, but also of shepherding them through the process of relationship dissolution, if it comes to that.

Applying this same logic to your relationship with your career, my first goal was to identify what the precipitating events are that make career goers contemplate going on the job market. In the first survey I conducted, I found there are five key drivers that make people think of leaving their jobs:

1. Feeling like their career is no longer an important part of who they are, when it used to be.

2. Working in a job that has changed so much it is now beyond recognition.

3. Taking on too much at work and feeling so overwhelmed that a feeling of helplessness is setting in.

4. Struggling to gain status at work, to the point where promotions and raises aren't being given.

5. Having power and status at work, but not getting recognized or compensated for it.

The chapters in this book are based on these five drivers, which I call: the Crisis of Identity, the Drifted Apart, the Stretched Too Thin, the Runner-Up, and the Underappreciated Star. Each chapter includes a unique set of data I collected on that type of career goer. To help you better understand your own situation, I probed into their psychological experiences, their behaviors at work, and who or what they thought was to blame for their current situation. And because this is a book about finding work that you love again or for the first time, I also collected data from people who hire, promote, and fire people. I interviewed career recruiters and hiring managers from a range of industries; I met with hiring experts who've mastered tools like LinkedIn Recruiter; and I spoke with seasoned leaders who've developed intricate interview practices designed to test the skills people use on the job. These people gave me insights into what questions people should be asking (but rarely do) in interviews, how to make a résumé more appealing, and with whom to network to learn insider secrets so that you may secure the job you desire most. Every type of career goer will face different hurdles during the application and interview process, from convincing a hiring manager that they can make a major career pivot, to detecting communication gaps between the person who's interviewing them for a job and the person who will eventually oversee them. To this end, each chapter contains bespoke advice designed to address the hurdles that are the most common among each type of career goer.

How you should read this book

One of the first questions people ask me when I tell them about the five types of career goer is "Which one am I?" The short answer is "Take my test and you'll find out." But the long answer is

"You might find that you aren't just one. Most people are two or three."

Because this book is organized around psychological profiles, not career types, the chapters are not mutually exclusive. You can certainly question how much you identify with your career and feel underappreciated at the same time. For this reason, I would think about them as most relevant to least relevant. I resonate most strongly with the Crisis of Identity career goer, but I also feel Stretched Too Thin sometimes, for example.

Before we dive into the quiz to help you figure out which types resonate the most with you, let's start with an overview of what each type is and what you'll find in each chapter.

THE CRISIS OF IDENTITY

The journey of the Crisis of Identity career goer can feel the most daunting of all those in this book. This person has spent months, often years, honing their skills and has a lot to show for it. They have well-developed professional networks and knowledge of the hidden curriculum. Their job is a core part of who they are, and their personal life and workplace life are often sewn together in an intricate web. Yet they question whether this career is right for them and fantasize about the chance to do something new and different. The Crisis of Identity career goer's journey begins with a little soul searching: Do you still feel like your old career is an important part of who you are, and how bad would you feel if you could never do it again? Only after processing the loss of their old identity can this career goer start building a new one. Because this career goer is wading into uncharted waters, this chapter covers a lot of ground. You will learn how to form connections with people outside your existing career network to learn things about your potential next career that aren't advertised on company websites—for example, hidden norms about the workplace, including what it takes to make a successful transition as an outsider, or the meaning of jargon and acronyms you're not familiar with but that are commonly used on résumés and in everyday workplace conversations. Think of this chapter as a starting place to build career-discovery skills.

THE DRIFTED APART

Many of us might have had the experience of looking at a longtime partner or close friend and thinking, "You've changed so much recently, I don't think I recognize the person you've become." Now imagine you have this sentiment about your job. The Drifted Apart know what it feels like to be happy at work—they know how to find purpose in their job, with whom to network for help, and what they need to do to perform well. But changes big and small have eaten away at the certainty they once felt. Their enjoyment in the job has been sapped; they don't feel confident in their ability to do their job well; and many have lost their drive to try. Their journey begins by understanding how widespread the changes they've experienced are: Is it the whole industry, their organization, or something more local—like their team or even their boss—changing that's at the heart of why things feel different?

And like all people in relationships who drift apart, they need to ask themselves, "How much of my unhappiness is because *I'm* the one who's changed?" The Drifted Apart experience changes in their daily lives—for example, a shift in how much time their boss gives them or a sudden increase in the number of new people put on their team—that are the result of bigger changes made behind closed doors. To see how these big changes impact the daily ones they feel, they need insights from a specific group of people: those who helped plan big changes *and* understand how these changes affect people's everyday work lives. The insights from the "planners" I surveyed are critical to building a list of job must-haves that are related to the realities of a changing workplace. For the interview process, I will teach you how to probe into the relationships between decision-makers and the people who oversee you. In constantly changing workplaces, these relationships are often obscured from view, and small things, like knowing whether your future boss was involved in the creation of the job advertisement you responded to (or has even seen it), can provide illuminating answers.

THE STRETCHED TOO THIN

If you've ever felt the exquisite torture of having to choose be-tween two things you love—a job opportunity in a new city and your relationship right here at home—or the low-level irritation of having to choose between two things that you don't love but need to get done—getting dinner on the table and finishing that report due tomorrow—then you can relate to this chapter. The feeling of being stretched too thin is so ubiquitous at work, I recommend this chapter for everyone who is feeling burned out, overworked, and exhausted by the pile of work on their desk that never seems to shrink.

The journey of the Stretched Too Thin career goer begins by answering two big questions: Am I taking on too many roles at work, like running a team while volunteering for a new committee? Am I switching between tasks so often that I never finish what I start? As I learned in my research for this chapter, some people are stretched too thin because they take on roles they aren't compensated for. In some workplaces, it's just the norm to do so (everyone is doing it); in others, people do it because they think it will increase their visibility at work and help them get ahead. Helping you learn which roles are worth it and which aren't is a major goal of this chapter, along with building strategies to protect your boundaries. To help the serial task switchers, I provide easy-to-use strategies for curbing the habit of starting one thing and changing quickly to another. To prevent a future life of being a Stretched Too Thin career goer, this chapter teaches you how to be an anthropologist of the workplace; you will learn how small things, like having an open floor plan, or working next to compared to twenty feet away from a coworker, can increase the likelihood that you'll wind up back here.

The strategies I cover in this chapter aren't just for people who are thinking of leaving a job; they are for everyone who struggles with the daily juggle. Think of it as a bonus add-on to the chapter that you most strongly resonate with.

THE RUNNER-UP

It doesn't matter how advanced you are in your career, the experience of missing that promotion or raise stings. No one enjoys coming in second (or third or fourth). We didn't like it when we played sports on the playground as kids, and we don't like it now. The Runner-Up knows who they are and where they want to go, but they struggle with a big piece of the puzzle: What have I been doing wrong? If you're anything like the Runners-Up I surveyed, you're not getting straightforward answers to this question; only 7 percent of people I studied were explicitly told why they failed to land a promotion or raise.

This chapter teaches you how to play detective to get the information you need. You will learn how to figure out how much status you have at work, and whether structural changes, like "jolts" to the workplace (big changes that shake things up), are to blame for your position. You will also learn norms around what roles and job duties people expect you to fill, even if they don't come out and say so. An important question the Runner-Up will need to answer is whether they need to take a step back before taking a step forward, filling in gaps in experience and job titles. Moving forward, this chapter teaches you how to test whether an organization has a culture of asking for and receiving clear feedback. Working for a company that can explain their feedback process is a must for the Runner-Up job seeker, down to what the daily or weekly structure of that feedback will be.

THE UNDERAPPRECIATED STAR

Have you ever felt like you put more into a relationship than you get out of it? That the hard work you do—planning date nights, running household errands, and making a real effort to stay attractive for your partner—is going unnoticed or underappreciated? Finding yourself underappreciated by a romantic partner can feel demoralizing, and the same is true at work. The Underappreciated Star feels a tension between what they give to their organization and what that organization gives back. Because they are arguably quite good at their jobs (an assumption that Underappreciated Stars should test), most are getting rewarded at work, but not in the ways they want. Hard work is often rewarded with more hard work, and raises are promises waived until some hypothetical future. The first goal of the Underappreciated Star is to learn their value in the marketplace by learning who their real competition is. Strategic networking will help with this process, which involves moving beyond local comparisons between yourself and your coworkers, to global comparisons between yourself and the people in your profession. Once you're ready to put yourself out there, you will need to find answers to questions like Do most companies really care about hiring stars, or is good enough just fine? There's a lot of evidence that some companies hire for "good enough" and aren't looking for stars, and that might be a barrier you will need to work around. This chapter builds on the tactics of the prior four, expanding on exercises you learned previously to help you find a job that will check off all your appreciation boxes.

WHAT TYPE OF CAREER GOER ARE YOU?

■ ■ ■

I designed this short quiz to help you get a sense of which type of career goer you might be. Read the questions below and answer each one. You should recognize the five drivers of change in these questions.

1. Are you thinking of leaving your career for a completely different one?

   ☐ yes   ☐ no

2. Is your current career an important part of who you are?

   ☐ yes   ☐ no

3. Did you used to love your job, but you no longer do?

   ☐ yes   ☐ no

4. If you answered yes to question 3, would you like to find a job that is similar to your old job, when you last enjoyed it?

   ☐ yes   ☐ no

5. Do you have multiple roles at work? These include job titles and any additional roles or responsibilities, such as being on a committee or in an employee resource group. If you do it at work, it counts.

   ☐ yes   ☐ no

6. Do you find yourself getting interrupted at work when you're trying to complete tasks?

   ☐ yes ☐ no

7. Do you feel stressed about the amount of work you don't get done by the end of the day?

   ☐ yes ☐ no

8. Are you currently employed and having a hard time landing a promotion?

   ☐ yes ☐ no

9. Do you feel like people with your level of performance who work for another company are better compensated than you?

   ☐ yes ☐ no

10. Do you feel like your effort goes unappreciated or unac- knowledged at work?

    ☐ yes ☐ no

11. Now think of some of your work skills. For each of them, ask yourself whether they are rare, whether they positively im- pact performance at work, and whether you are better at them than other people. Do you have at least one skill that fits all those criteria?

    ☐ yes ☐ no

Answer Key:

■ If you answered *yes* to 1, you're probably a Crisis of Identity career goer. If you also answered *yes* to 2, then you might not be ready to leave that career yet, but this chapter is still for you.

■ But if you answered *no* to 1, and *yes* to 3 or 4, then the Drifted Apart chapter is for you.

■ If you answered *yes* to 5, 6, or 7, then the Stretched Too Thin chapter is for you.

■ If you answered *yes* to 8 or 9, then you're a Runner-Up.

■ And if you answered *yes* to 9 or 10, and *yes* to 11, then you're likely an Underappreciated Star.

Which categories are the most common?

Across four hundred people I interviewed in nine countries and twenty-two industries, about 41 percent identified as Crisis of Identity, 28 percent as Drifted Apart, 35 percent as Stretched Too Thin, and 42 percent as Runner-Ups or Underappreciated Stars. Remember, people can belong to more than one category—the average was about two. Stretched Too Thin was the second category for most people.

Most people are many things, as you probably are.

Given that you're probably more than one type, how should

you approach this book? In what order should you read these chapters if you're more than one type? I say start with what interests you the most.

I designed *Job Therapy* to be readable in any order, meaning you can start with whatever chapter most resonates with you, then go back and read the others. Think of the book like a game with multiple worlds that don't need to be played in order. The adventures you go on are different, and so, too, are the contexts and settings. But the levels of the worlds are structured in the same way, and all worlds play by the same rules.

To that end, each chapter in this book is organized around four stages:

Why Am I Unhappy?	What Do I Want My Future Career to Look Like?	Fact-Finding to See If the Job Is the Right Fit for Me	Securing the Job
Identify the psychological source of your unhappiness with self-assessment tools	Learn whom to network with and what to ask your new network connections	Learn what questions to ask during the interview process	Learn how to craft a résumé and ask the right questions during the interview to land the job

The chapters open with stage one: understanding why you're unhappy at work. This stage includes a set of assessments that dig deeper into the psychology behind the type of career goer that the chapter is about. Stage two is focused on what you want your future career to look like. This stage is meant to be worked through before you start applying for jobs. In most chapters it is largely focused on whom you should network with to ask the questions that don't have easy-to-find answers on company websites—questions that require you to go behind the scenes a bit to get the answers you need. Stage three is about how to go on a fact-finding mission to test whether a career or job is a good fit for you. This stage focuses on the application and interview processes. I draw from interviews with recruiters and hiring managers to create a structured list of questions for you to ask. Stage four is about securing the job. Often this stage is worked on concurrently with stage three. It focuses on topics like how to frame your skills without overselling them, and what questions to ask during the interview to signal your long-term commitment to a job.

You can toggle among chapters—comparing your stage-one progress if you feel Stretched Too Thin to your stage-one progress if you're a Runner-Up, for example. There is only one real either-or decision you need to make when reading this book: Do you want to transition to an entirely different career, or do you want to stay the course with the one you have? If you've identified as a Crisis of Identity career goer—you're thinking of leaving your career to try something different—I suggest starting your journey with chapter 1. Everyone else can start anywhere.

Tessa's stress test

Before you read this book you need to learn what triggers your stress at work. I discovered that the things that make people unhappy at work are often small and forgettable, but add up over time—daily stressors that we quickly forget about, like a commuter train that gets stuck on the tracks, making us late to a meeting, or an unfinished to-do list that we sit thinking about over dinner with our family. Often, we don't experience their effects until days, even weeks, later, when we miss a good night's sleep and wind up with a cold.

Occasionally, I reference this stress test, which is a short quiz that you can take every day for a few days in a row, or for a whole week or longer, to document your stressors. To design the test, I spoke with social psychologist Dr. Amie Gordon, who's an expert in measuring people's daily experiences to understand what their biggest stressors are. From Amie's perspective, one of the most important things to do is to document what you think will stress you out each day and, at the end of the day, write down what actually stressed you out. There are often big discrepancies between these things, but if we rely on memory alone, we get pulled toward what she calls "peak experiences"—big, stressful events that we clearly remember, like a high-stakes presentation. But if you look at people's daily data, the events we dread the most aren't actually that bad. It's the ones we didn't anticipate that add up, stressing us out more than we realize. Amie's been surprised at how often.

The test is simple. There is one question you will answer in the morning before work, and a handful of questions you will need to answer at night before you go to bed.

DAILY STRESS TEST

In the morning before work, answer this one question:

In thinking about your day, what are you the most worried about?

In the evening right before bed, answer these questions:

Think back on your day and zero in on the very worst part of it—the part of your day when you were unhappy, stressed, angry, bored, frustrated, overwhelmed, or simply just trying to get to the next thing. Think about that time for a few minutes and answer the following questions:

DESCRIBE THE EVENT

What time of day was it? Time _____ a.m./p.m.

Where were you?

☐ At home
☐ At work
☐ At leisure/having fun

☐ Running errands
☐ Traveling
☐ Other

Who were you with? (check all that apply)

☐ No one
☐ Strangers
☐ Coworkers
☐ Friends

☐ My children
☐ Significant other
☐ Other family
☐ Pets

Was this the same situation that you were the most worried about this morning?

☐ Yes ☐ No

How familiar or typical was this situation for you?

☐ First time   ☐ Do it regularly
☐ Done it once before   ☐ Do it all the time
☐ Done it a few times

How negative or positive did you feel during the situation you were worried about this morning?

☐ Not all negative   ☐ Somewhat positive
☐ Somewhat negative   ☐ Very positive
☐ Neutral   ☐ It didn't happen

How negative or positive did you feel during the situation you reported on this evening?

☐ Not all negative   ☐ Somewhat positive
☐ Somewhat negative   ☐ Very positive
☐ Neutral

WHAT DID I LEARN FROM THE PEOPLE WHO TOOK THE STRESS TEST?

I had fifty people take the test and the results were surprising.

To begin, about half the things people anticipated in the morning would be the worst parts of their day were not the same events they reported as stressful in the evening. On average, the anticipated morning events were negative for about half of the people (52 percent). The rest found them to be either positive (20 percent) or neutral (16 percent) or noted that the event didn't happen at all (12 percent). In line with Amie's experiences, often the anticipated stressors turn out to be not that bad.

Not surprisingly, most of the stressful events reported at the end of the day happened at work (66 percent), followed by at home (22 percent). And although these events were pretty negative—84 percent of people reported them as at least moderately stressful—they were also fairly mundane: not meeting deadlines, failing to complete tasks on time, rushing to get everything on their to-do list accomplished; the type of events that put people in the Stretched Too Thin category.

HOW EXPERIENCED ARE WE WITH OUR UNANTICIPATED STRESSORS?

Here's where things get a little surprising. These events did not come out of the blue. Around 72 percent of people have gone through the "unanticipated stressor" at least a few times, and among those, 34 percent do it fairly regularly! The events that turn out to be the most stressful for us are often regular occurrences. So why are we so bad at anticipating them?

Experiencing a routine stressor can lead you to become desensitized to it; you no longer recognize the physiologic pattern in your body as a stress response. It's a bit like having a nightly fight with your spouse over how next month's bills are going to get paid. You do it so often, you don't realize that your blood pressure spikes for a solid twenty minutes between 8:00 and 10:00 p.m. every night.

If you want to learn what types of things get your heart racing at work, I recommend you take the stress test every day for at least a few days in a row, or to get a more comprehensive understanding of your stress patterns, a week or longer. Keep in mind that the answers might surprise you. You might find that despite routinely dealing with picking up the slack for a coworker, it's still the biggest source of stress you encounter each day. And the good news is that once you have a sense of what triggers your stress at work, you can ask questions during stages two and three to find out whether a workplace is a good stress fit for you.

A few last tips

Before you dive in, it can be helpful to learn a few hacks that will make the process of finding a new job easier no matter what type of career goer you are. Two of the most important ones are: What should I say when I reach out to strangers? What's the best way to strategically apply for jobs?

WHAT SHOULD I SAY WHEN I REACH OUT TO STRANGERS?

Networking, in the world of work, is like breathing. All the hiring experts I interviewed highlighted how important it is for landing a job—tomorrow or ten years from now. Each chapter gives you specific advice on whom to network with and what specific questions you should ask during your conversations. But unless you know the person, it can be very awkward to say, "You don't know me, but any chance we can chat about your career?"

To help guide you, I asked four hundred people what would increase the likelihood that they would respond to a request to have a career chat with a stranger. The good news is, 51 percent said they would do it, but under specific conditions. It's best if you have a shared network connection, and it doesn't need to be a person; belonging to the same group on social media can work (career groups on LinkedIn or other workplace sites work well). Reach out over email or LinkedIn (not on their personal social media account), and in your message tell the person how you found them so it doesn't feel like spam ("I found you in a search for people who work in STEM," for example). Mention a few things about them personally ("I noticed you worked for such-and-such company about five years ago"), give them a list of questions you want to ask (I recommend bullet points to keep it short), and request a fifteen-minute chat, on Zoom or the phone. And whatever you do, don't send them a calendar invite before they've responded, and don't ask for an hour-long call. And that's it! Follow these basic steps and you'll be well on your way to building a rich new social network.

WHAT'S THE BEST WAY TO STRATEGICALLY APPLY FOR JOBS?

In my networking conversations with hiring managers and recruiters, there was one thing they all agreed on: People are applying for *way* too many jobs.

RecruitingDaily.com president and influencer William Tincup put it bluntly: "If you're applying for a thousand jobs, you're failing." Batch applying is easier now than ever; it often comes down to the click of a button. But when we take a more-is-more approach, we often skip the hard steps: tailoring our materials to the job description, connecting with current employees to learn more about the company, even visiting the company website to find out what they do. I asked two hundred people who hire for a living, "When applying for jobs, people should . . . ," followed by a list of practices. Here are the five most recommended ones, with the percentage of people who endorsed it:

- Send a tailored résumé to each job (91 percent)

- Include company outcomes you contributed to on your résumé (86 percent)

- Include all your certifications, degrees, and languages spoken (between 83 percent and 94 percent across these three things)

- Use a tailored cover letter (73 percent)

- Use words or phrases from a job description on a résumé (72 percent)

With these tips in your back pocket, you're ready to go! Good luck on your journey, and remember, keep the answers to your stress test handy as you move through this book. It's just as important that you find a job that fits your career needs as it is to find one that allows you to keep your stress levels in check.

Job Therapy

THE CRISIS OF IDENTITY

*I thought this career was for me,
but now I'm having second thoughts*

I sat down with Timothy, a technology expert who's been at the same company for the past eight years. In preparation for this interview, I told him I thought he'd be perfect for the chapter on a type of career goer called the Crisis of Identity—the person who's spent years perfecting their skills but has ambivalent feelings about their career and sometimes contemplates leaving it.

Within moments of the interview, I began to question my judgment. "I know what this chapter is about, and I am not the ideal candidate to interview for it," he tells me right out the gate.

"I've been the go-to guy for helping people with technology since high school," he says, followed by a passionate take on how "technology [is the] underpinning of every function of society." If Timothy's trying to shatter my assumption that he's not dedicated to the craft anymore, he's doing a good job. Plus, there's the small issue of his having no immediate plans to leave his job and not even really looking.

But over the course of our forty-five-minute conversation, I become convinced that Tim is indeed questioning his identity.

There's an ambivalence in his assertions that perfectly captures the complexity of the Crisis of Identity career goer. People like him don't experience their change in career engagement in black and white—that is, they aren't committed workaholics one day, quiet quitters the next. They're in love with their jobs and in hate with them, often at the same time. Their feelings are messy and often take a long time to unravel or process.

For Tim, much of this messiness stems from the complicated relationship he has with his organization.

Like many organizations, Tim's office was experiencing a low-level malaise that had spread through the workplace like a virus. People stopped coming in, and in his line of work, the job can't be done entirely remotely (tech in conference rooms needed to be set up in person—with someone physically there to attach wires and check on the software, for example). As a consequence, mistakes were made and a lot of people either left or were laid off. Tim, who prides himself on never having caught this virus, left his role, searching for greener pastures. He wanted to be around colleagues who brought energy to the workplace. Or at least who were willing to come in.

But when he moved to a different branch of the organization, situated in a different building, all he found was more malaise and more unmotivated people. It was dawning on him that perhaps all information technology (IT) offices are like this—that the era of engaged tech experts is long gone.

I saw small clues that he was starting to question how this reality might affect his identity as a person who loves a career in technology. He casually brings up the possibility of moving to another state and working in higher education (which would require a trip back to school). But when I ask him about how serious he is about a career change, he waves me away. "That's for when I'm much older," he tells me.

During our interview I witnessed Tim oscillate between dreaming of a different career and leveling up at the one he has. Of starting over completely and of getting that big promotion he's always dreamed of. From my perspective, Tim is in the nascent stage of an identity crisis. There are some cracks, but nothing has broken yet. There are still enough good days to keep him coming back to work. But he is ultimately questioning whether a job in technology, which he's always prided himself on, is right for him anymore.

Others I spoke with are much further along in their journey. Susan—a professor turned UX researcher—had an experience very similar to Timothy's a few years before she decided to make a big career move. She had tenure at a university and was fully committed to her career in academia.

But her job changed starkly during the pandemic, morphing into a form she didn't recognize. The recession meant layoffs and unwanted changes coming from the top down, including change to who taught the courses she regularly taught. And with shifting standards came a change in herself she didn't recognize: a sudden loss of self-efficacy. No matter how hard she worked, it did not seem to matter. Despite being a top performer her whole life, the disengagement around her started to eat away at her confidence. "I was unsure of my value, even though I had accomplished a lot in my life and I was proud of the things I'd done," she told me. Susan made me realize that you don't need to be failing at work to have an identity crisis. Many transitioners like Susan and Timothy are doing quite well, but either they aren't recognized by others for their hard work, or the recognition no longer makes them feel good about themselves. The dopamine boosts have stopped coming.

Once she no longer felt like being a professor was an important part of her identity—a process that took time and a lot of networking to figure out—Susan was methodical in her career transition. In fact, many of the steps I recommend you work through were inspired by Susan's journey. She spent time networking with people outside her profession as an academic, learning how to frame her skills in new ways that often surprised her. She learned how and when to speak like an insider, which helped her develop her new career identity. And she learned which jargon phrases and acronyms were appropriate for her résumé. These small acquisitions of new knowledge added up, and eventually she landed her dream job.

What is a Crisis of Identity career goer?

This chapter isn't about people afraid of dedicating themselves to one career, or people who don't mind a few twists and turns on the path toward career discovery. It's about focused career goers who've had their hearts set for years on making it at one profession—people who've felt their personal identity shaped by their career, and who aren't the type to impulsively leave it. They have built their identity around what they do or what their job title is. Many are far enough along in their careers to have made it through the early weeding-out process, and some, like Susan and Timothy, have enviable skill sets. They've climbed to the upper rungs of their path, but then the doubts crept in.

The decision to leave is a tough one, perhaps the toughest of all the hurdles faced by the job seekers I cover in this book. It can affect your relationships outside work, especially if the career you now hold pays well and people are dependent on you for their livelihood. Susan got pushback from her immigrant parents, who spent decades making sure their children had opportunities they didn't. They were shocked that she would deviate from a path with a guaranteed steady income. Another transitioner told me that her partner accused her of being "irresponsible, selfish, and capricious." Her partner's job had paid for her student loans, and they had just finished paying them off. "But I couldn't stop the nagging question in the back of my mind, 'Is this really what I want to do with the rest of my life?'" she told me. Living with existential angst wasn't sustainable, so she quit before landing a new job.

I've talked to dozens of people who were facing a crisis of identity at work, some of whom were so terrified of making a mistake by leaving that they spent a good number of waking hours "job lurking" instead. Most followed a three-step process: scrolling through job ads and falling in love with a dream job, finding out who got the dream job, and then stalking the person online to learn about their qualifications and career trajectory. Few actually took the next step and reached out to these people to network with them. It's a bit like getting on the dating apps and never actually going out with anyone you match with. It feels like a step in the right direction, but in the end you're still sitting at home, afraid of putting yourself out there. The first stage of this book is about breaking the cycle of fantasizing about another career.

Stage one: Why am I unhappy here? Learn your psychological starting place

For people who are struggling with their identity at work, there's a critical question they need to ask themselves before they leave their current job: Am I truly ready to leave this career?

Psychological readiness is a complex topic. It requires you to understand your feelings of attachment to your current profession (and current workplace) before you can move on to a new career. To start this process, the first thing you need to do is evaluate how strongly you identify with your current career and with the place where you work.

How strong is my current career identity?

I asked *The Power of Us* author Jay J. Van Bavel, who studies the ways our identities shape our thoughts and behaviors, why identity matters so much at work. Jay has conducted dozens of studies showing how strongly held identities can lead people to engage in all sorts of behaviors, good and bad. Identity can explain why people believe in conspiracy theories and join cults (as examples of the bad), as well as why they stay motivated at work and, in some cases, have a hard time leaving jobs they no longer enjoy.

I asked him if there's a way for people to gain insight into the strength of their own workplace identities, and whether there are signs they can recognize in themselves that a workplace identity has started to wane.

The first step, he told me, is to try to understand which identities are at play. "People are often not aware of their identities, but they constrain how you think, how you behave, and who you connect with. At work, two identities are relevant. First, you need to ask yourself, do you have an organizational identity? If you do, that might make it hard to leave for another organization, even if you plan to keep your profession. Second, do you identify with your role or profession?"

It might seem strange, but it's possible to have a strong organizational identity (you love your company) even if you don't have a strong professional one, especially if you have a lot of close relationships at work: people you'd like to stay in touch with even if you make a radical career change. As you start contemplating an exit, take some time to evaluate how strongly you identify with your current career. On the next page are questions that Colin Wayne Leach, an identity expert and professor of psychology, developed. With these questions, he measures two components of identity: *identity centrality*, or how central your career identity is to you, and *identity satisfaction*, or how much joy your identity brings you. Both types of identity are important for figuring out what you want your future career to look like, and they tend to operate independently of each other. It's possible, for example, to feel highly identified with your career (it's a big part of how you define yourself) even if it brings you very little satisfaction.

Insert your profession in the blanks on the next page and rate each of these statements from a 1 (not at all) to 5 (very much) scale.

These statements capture your *identity centrality*:

A. I often think about the fact that I am a ⬚

1 2 3 4 5

B. Being a ⬚
is an important part of how I see myself.

1 2 3 4 5

These statements capture *identity satisfaction*:

C. I am glad to be a ⬚

1 2 3 4 5

D. I think that ⬚
have a lot to be proud of.

1 2 3 4 5

E. It is pleasant to be a ⬚

1 2 3 4 5

F. Being a ⬚
gives me a good feeling.

1 2 3 4 5

The first time you take this test, answer both sets of questions twice: once for your career (for example, "creative director"), and once for your workplace, switching out the job title for the company ("Disney employee"). If you see that you have strong identity centrality and strong identity satisfaction with your career but weak centrality and satisfaction with the place you work, you might be less of a Crisis of Identity career goer than you think. As covered in the next chapter on the Drifted Apart, sometimes we feel so negative about our jobs that our feelings of discontent spread to every facet of our working lives, from how we feel sitting in traffic to the promotion structure of the organization. Your goal here is to make sure that you aren't mistaking a low identity with your organization for a low identity with your career. It would be a shame to ditch a career you still identify with simply because you hate the place you work.

Once you've taken both parts of the test (identity centrality and identity satisfaction), you will need to create two separate scores (by summing your total score and dividing by the number of items—2 for identity centrality and 4 for identity satisfaction). An average score of 3 or below (out of 5) means that you're scoring relatively low on the measure because 3 is the midpoint, and a score of 4 or above means that you're scoring relatively high.

For example, here are my answers:

A. I often think about the fact that I am a professor of psychology. (4)

B. Being a psychology professor is an important part of how I see myself. (5)

C. I am glad to be a psychology professor. (4)

D. I think that psychology professors have a lot to be proud of. (4)

E. It is pleasant to be a psychology professor. (3)

F. Being a psychology professor gives me a good feeling. (5)

Identity centrality = (Answers from A + B) ÷ 2

Mine is: (4+5) ÷ 2 = 4.5, or relatively high

Identity satisfaction = (Answers from C + D + E + F) ÷ 4

Mine is: (4 + 4 + 3 + 5) ÷ 4 = 4, or relatively high

Don't forget to fill in the blanks again for your workplace.

After you've taken this test, you might be wondering, "How do I score relative to others who are thinking of leaving their careers?" I surveyed two hundred people who were thinking of leaving their careers or were in the process of transitioning out of their careers. In analyzing people's career centrality and career satisfaction, I observed that on average people scored either high on each of these measures (above a 3) or low (below a 3); few were in the middle of the scale. Based on this observation, I created four different categories:

Many of the people (38 percent) in this study are high on both identity centrality and satisfaction—**Thrivers**. This is fascinating, given that I selected people for this study who were thinking of leaving their careers. Timothy, who entertains the idea of leaving but quickly swings back to defending his decision to stay, likely

IDENTITY SATISFACTION

		HIGH	LOW
IDENTITY CENTRALITY	**HIGH**	THRIVERS 38%	DIE HARDERS 20%
	LOW	HAPPY DISTANCERS 13%	GET-ME-OUTERS 29%

falls into this category. If this is you, you might have measured your identity on a "good day," when things were looking up at work. Later, I talk about the importance of repeating the test to look for stability in your score before you make a big move. If, however, you have a strong, stable identity, you probably fall into one of the other types of career goers I talk about in the book, those who want to stay in their industry, but not their job (Underappreciated Stars and Runners-Up fall into this category).

Get-Me-Outers are 29 percent of the people in this study. Low on both identity centrality and satisfaction, these people have moved on psychologically from their careers. There are a lot of practical reasons why they might not be ready to leave, but the fear of losing a part of themselves in the process isn't one of them. It's a bit like staying in a cohabitating relationship for purely practical reasons—rent in two places is too expensive; we have a dog

and who would get it? In romantic relationships, the pull of prac-
ticality often keeps people tethered to each other for years after
the spark is gone. At work, stability in your situation—whether that
is a predictable workday, a good paycheck, or knowing that your
head won't be on the chopping block anytime soon—acts like invisible glue, tethering you to a career you neither love nor care
about.

Happy Distancers, at 13 percent, are perfectly satisfied with
their identities, they just don't see their (or these) identities as
central to who they are as people. Many of us can go merrily along
in life with a job that doesn't define us. If you're a Happy Distancer
the question you want to ask yourself is this: Do you *need* your
career to feed into your identity, or are there other sources of
identity that get the job done just fine? Not everyone derives a
sense of purpose from work, but not everyone is looking to. But if
you work in a profession where you're *expected* to have a strong
workplace identity—where you're punished, even, for not—then
the mismatch between you and those around you can cause tension. I felt this way about a past job in retail. Everyone was into
the team-building exercises and inter-store sales competitions
except me; I was just there to make money. It was awkward going
to work and dealing with the eye rolls.

The trickiest category to fall into is the **Die Harder**, which makes
up 20 percent of my sample. I feel for these people. They rarely get
pleasure from their workplace identity, but it's still core to who
they are. They both hate and love the ride, and most have been
suffering for so long that they've gotten used to it. If you've ever
felt yourself working tirelessly on vacation despite being bitter the

entire time, or taking on responsibility after responsibility not because you enjoy the work but because turning them down makes you feel like a failure, then you probably fall into this category.

MEASURE YOUR IDENTITY MULTIPLE TIMES, NOT JUST ONCE

Identity is a complex thing, often waxing and waning over time. Change in the strength of our workplace identities is often nonlinear, characterized by peaks and sudden drops rather than a steady decline. Some people feel the drop in identity satisfaction long before they feel a drop in identity centrality, falling into the category of Die Harder before they become a Get-Me-Outer. People in health care, who've been suffering from burnout at exceedingly high rates, often are in this category. Many are deeply committed to the job but struggle with the intense stress they experience.

Old identities die hard, and the Crisis of Identity career transitioners I interviewed often talked about their old professions like people talk about a troublesome romantic relationship: things were hot, then cold, then hot again. It's hard to get off the emotional roller coaster. Asking yourself the question "Is my career identity gone for good?" can feel existential. "Many people who leave their careers don't understand the identity part until right up to the point where they need to let it go. And the letting go part can be downright agonizing," Jay Van Bavel told me.

For this reason, it's important to measure identity strength repeatedly over the course of a few months, starting from the moment when you begin contemplating an exit. Don't make a radical change based on a single data point; make it based on a consistent pattern of change. By nature our identities aren't static, and you might be tempted to read too much into a "bad identity" day. A momentary cue can activate an identity or threaten it. One day, your boss might praise you for your good work and your identity goes up; the next, you're slammed with more requests than you can handle and it drops again.

To help with this process, I recommend using the same window of time in which you complete the identity measure on page 8 to retake the Daily Stress Test introduced on page xxix. If you do this, you will gain insight into what factors co-occur with fluxes and flows in identity. Ask yourself: What stressors (anticipated or not) trigger shifts in the strength of your identity? Common ones include a failure to get recognized for your contributions, changing standards and rules that pop up unexpectedly, and environmental cues, like working in a completely empty office or an overcrowded one.

Recognizing what co-occurs with shifts in the strength of your identity—like a particular relationship dynamic that triggers stress, or a long stretch of working with disengaged team members—can give you important insights into what you want your future career to look like. Imagine, for example, that you experienced your identity centrality and satisfaction drop when you stopped getting recognized for your contributions at work. You want strong workplace recognition to be a goal moving forward so you don't find yourself having another identity crisis at your next job.

> ## My identity with my career has been low for a long time. What should I do next?

If you've seen a consistent drop in your identity centrality and identity satisfaction, ask yourself one last question before you move on: How bad would you feel if you couldn't do this job anymore?

This question, which is important for gauging readiness to leave a job, can spark some emotions in you that you might not yet have processed, including the fear of failure. This fear can lead people to do funny things, like going "all in" at work in a final, last-ditch effort to prove to yourself that you did everything you could to make it work. Susan, for example, spent a lot of time volunteering to help other professors just before she quit. Anyone who's been in relationship counseling just before a divorce can relate to this experience. I think I went on more date nights with my ex-husband in the two months leading up to our separation than I did during the whole marriage!

As you work through stage one, remind yourself that it's okay to have ambivalent feelings about your current career. Exploring options, which you will do in stage two, is not the same thing as leaving. You will find moving forward that small, meaningful interactions with people in your potential new profession will help you process the loss of your old identity as you start to build a new one. These interactions can be done at any pace you feel comfortable with.

Stage two: What do I want my future career to look like?

For people who are experiencing an identity change, the second stage of their career transition—figuring out what they want their future career to look like—can feel daunting. Questions like "What should my new identity be when I don't know what the possibilities are?" and "How am I supposed to know what's out there when I've spent the last several years of my life dedicated to one thing?" are common at this stage. And so, too, is feeling a bit of career paralysis: you know what you *don't* like to do, but you have no idea what you might actually enjoy. Since you're so familiar with what went wrong in the past, you might be tempted to make a list of "don'ts"—things you definitely want to avoid in the future.

Focusing on key differences between your old career and your future one will be important, but I urge you not to start there. Instead, try a different approach: Don't think about what you want to do that's different from your current career. Think about what you want to do that's *the same*.

BUILD A LIST OF KEEPER SKILLS

To do this, you will need to start by building a list of keeper skills: things that you're good at and want to bring with you to your next career. There's an art to this process. As I learned from the job seekers I studied for this chapter, small differences in how you frame your skills can make a big difference not only in how interested you are in using them again, but also in how you talk about how to transfer those skills to a new profession during your networking conversations.

Let me illustrate with a short exercise.

Three Things Exercise

1. What is a task you do at work?

2. What is the skill required to execute that task?

3. What is the context in which the task is done?

Now complete this exercise five times, to capture five different tasks, skills, and contexts. I call this the Three Things Exercise.

I had one hundred people who are thinking of changing careers go through this exercise, and I compared their answers to those from another hundred people who completed a simpler version, in which I asked them to write out "five different skills you have." I'll call this the skills only group. It's common for recruiters and hirers who work with career transitioners to ask, "What skills do you have that you want to bring with you to your next career?" Most won't ask you to break your answer down into the task you're doing in which that skill is applied, or the context in which you're doing it.

In comparing these two groups, I found that framing had a huge impact on people's answers. By and large, the skills only group listed skills that were so general, they felt more like personality traits than skills you execute on the job: adaptive, agile, a good problem solver, attentive to detail, for example. In contrast, the people who did the Three Things Exercise were much more specific in their answers, focusing on concrete skills that belong on a résumé. For example, a sales administrator wrote "distributing the day's workload" for the task, "using advanced Microsoft Office" for the skill, and "in a crowded office" for the context.

Once you have a list of your specific skills at this stage—whether they are working with Microsoft Word or developing tests for grade-three students—start thinking about which of those skills you want to bring with you to your next career. Having specific skills in mind will help you get concrete answers out of your network connections to the question "How can I translate a skill from my past career to a new one?" For example, if someone were to come to me and say, "I was agile and a good problem solver in my last career. Are those skills relevant to being a professor?" I would say, "Of course! Positive traits like these are always a good thing." But if they came to me and instead asked, "I'm a whiz at Microsoft Office. Is this a skill I can use as a professor?" I would have a much more thoughtful answer, grounded in the reality of everyday life as a professor. The Three Things Exercise also helps you think concretely about what you do and don't want your daily life at work to look like moving forward. You might realize, for example, that you love using Microsoft Office, but you want to move beyond the clerical work of distributing the day's workload. And you hate crowded offices. Knowing which of these three things you want to keep—including where you want to work or what kind of people you want to work with (if any!)—will help you fine-tune your career search.

GET CLARITY AROUND WHAT YOU WANT YOUR NEW CAREER IDENTITY TO BE

Now that your list of keeper skills is well under way, the next step is to develop clarity around where you want to go. Don't worry, this step doesn't require you to get a new job (or even apply for one). It does, however, require you to network with people who have insider information about the potential new identities you're exploring. The best way to start developing a new identity is to have a series of short, scheduled conversations to learn what the day-to-day looks like in different jobs. Later, I detail what your networking strategy should be to schedule these chats, but let's start with concrete examples of what clear and unclear identities at work look like.

▪ ▪ ▪

Social scientists Shoshana Dobrow and Monica Higgins observed 136 career goers over the course of five years, documenting the ways in which their career identities took shape. As part of their study, they collected samples of people's descriptions of their own career identities to see whether identity clarity predicted success at work.

Here's an example of a person with a clear career identity from their study:

Although I am positive that I would like to have a career in real estate . . . [t]raditionally, it has been difficult to enter and to exit the real estate industry. Now is the perfect time to strengthen my experience in the industry. My professional history clearly points in the direction of real estate.

The person in this example doesn't exactly know *how* to become a real estate agent—and they anticipate some barriers to success—but they know that they definitely want to be one. Importantly, having a strong career identity means you know what you want to be, but not necessarily how to get there. It's okay to start your exploration before you know the "how" piece. That's what networking is for.

Here's an example of a person with unclear career identity:

I'm having a hard time narrowing my focus into a specific role. I am considering jobs in marketing for "lifestyle" companies like media, entertainment, fashion, or cosmetics . . . or working in the arts so that I can have enough free time to continue my work on [my entrepreneurial venture] . . . or at an auction house . . . or in new product development within a creative company. I know I want to be at a place where I can learn and grow, but I'm very nervous about taking the first step and winding up going in the wrong direction.

This person knows very broadly what they are interested in, but at this point, they're entertaining several different options that are only tangentially related. Fashion, cosmetics, and entertainment might feel like they all fall under the same umbrella of lifestyle companies, but they require very different skill sets and entail different tasks. Wanting to "learn and grow" sounds nice, but it's vague.

You might feel more like the second person at this stage—you have a broad list of things that may or may not be related to one another that you're interested in pursuing, and that's okay. To help kick-start the identity-formation process, treat your list of keeper skills from stage one as a starter kit, along with the answers to your Three Things Exercise. Learning how your keeper skills are applied to new tasks and contexts should be your first goal during networking.

NETWORKING FOR IDENTITY BUILDING

Shoshana Dobrow and Monica Higgins didn't only measure how people described their identities in their study; they also collected data on who was able to create clear identities and find a job that fit them. Not all successful people were on a linear career path, and many of them redefined their identities a few times. But no matter what direction they went in, the ones who were able to find the answer to the question "Who do I want to be moving forward?" climbed up (and often out) at work. To get there, they used their social networks. In fact, one-on-one conversations did a lot more to help people refine their identities than building new skills, taking classes, getting new certifications, and reading books.

If you're established in your career, you probably already have a lot of networking skills. Most people who've been working in one career for a long time have what scientists refer to as a "dense" network—a lot of connections with people who work in the same organization, or with people who are in the same profession. I conducted a study with one hundred people who were thinking of transitioning from an established career to a new one. I asked these people to list ten names of people they knew through their career, including how they knew them. This method doesn't capture people's entire social network, but it gives us an idea of the type of people we're connected to. I found that more than half their connections—over six out of ten—were with people who worked at the same company as they did. A little more than four out of ten were from the same field or the same team. In total, nearly three quarters of people's connections—74 percent—were with people in their current industry. I also asked people whether (and how) their connections knew one another. Almost all shared connections worked for the same organization; they knew one another because they saw one another at work every day. By and large, we don't venture far from our current companies when it comes to forming social networks at work.

WHO SHOULD YOU BE NETWORKING WITH, INSTEAD OF PEOPLE AT YOUR COMPANY?

To develop a clear new identity, you will need to develop a broader, less career-centric social network. Meeting people at work is natural, but to make a career pivot, you will need to create a new network made up of people who have different experiences, work at different companies, and have different job titles. In short, your goal is to go after nonoverlapping information from your network connections.

This approach might go against your intuition. Shouldn't you want to be connected with people who know one another and can help you get a new job? Eventually, but not yet. At this stage, the more information overlap there is among people, the more you will assume that you have a clear picture of what a career looks like, when in reality you have a biased, thin-slice picture of a career. You might also assume that their shared experiences say something about the career these people have in common, when in reality it says something about their shared boss, office environment, or even something as simple as the number of days off people get.

If your connections have weak or no ties to one another, you will get a lot of different answers to questions about what it takes to succeed, whether your keeper skills are valued, and what the day-to-day looks like for different careers you're interested in. The benefits of a diverse network in which not everyone knows one another are far reaching. Dobrow and Higgins found that people who had less-dense networks in the first two years after getting their MBA also had clearer career identities four years later. Having a variety of information from different sources helped them fine-tune their identities.

TO FORM THESE CONNECTIONS, SEEK OUT PEOPLE FROM NONOVERLAPPING CAREER GROUPS

In the Dobrow and Higgins study, the people with the clearest identities had people in their network who didn't know one another, and who came from very different social groups: a past employer, a college friend, someone they met at a conference, and someone they knew from their community, for example. To create a network like this one, start by tapping into your existing networks, but make sure new connections aren't in the same industry or working for the same company. Many of the hiring experts I interviewed recommend using networks that are broad, like a network of fellow immigrants (if you are one) or an alumni network, as a starting place. It's okay to have networks that are identity-based (being first generation or recently immigrated, or going to the same university) as long as the identity people share isn't with the same company.

If you've narrowed your future job to a broad category (for example, customer service or something in STEM), you can network with people who have an overarching identity in common that encompasses different career identities. For example, people who use Salesforce have their own large networking community. Women in STEM have their own community (and you can find these groups easily on social media). People within these groups often want to see one another succeed and are willing to give newcomers the inside scoop.

HOW CAN I FORM THESE NETWORK CONNECTIONS?

To accomplish your networking goals, you will need to give up on the most common networking technique most of us rely on to meet new people: snowball sampling. If you've asked a network connection, "Do you know of anyone else I can speak to about this career?" then you've snowballed.

Snowballing is asking one network connection to recommend someone else in their network. By design, it means creating a network that is dense—the people within it know one another. But you don't need to start entirely from scratch; there are ways you can ask your current connections for recommendations that reduce the likelihood that people are connected through their jobs. For example, you could say, "Do you know of any other companies that have good reputations for catering?" instead of "Do you know of anyone else in catering whom I can reach out to?" It's a subtle difference, but it can lead to very different networking outcomes. As I mentioned in the opening, people are much more willing to talk to strangers about their careers than we think they are. So don't be too worried about rejection at this stage.

To keep yourself on track, have daily networking goals. For example, each day reach out to two people in your network who don't work for the same company to set up a career conversation. And remember, your goal isn't to have a huge network, it's to have a carefully crafted one. Two or three well-chosen connections will do a lot more for your identity development than ten connections chosen because they all worked with a friend of yours.

WHAT SHOULD I ASK DURING THESE CHATS?

When you first start out, you might feel unsure of how to keep track of what you've learned so you can consolidate it later. I recommend creating a worksheet that documents the relationship between the skills needed for these jobs and how these skills are executed by the people you're talking with. In other words, get your network connections to answer your Three Things Exercise. You can start by asking people, "I'm curious what your day-to-day is like. Would you mind walking me through a few tasks that you do each day?" Then you can probe for the skills needed to do these tasks with simple follow-ups.

As you go through this exercise, keep in mind your daily stressors from the stress test. Below is an example from an elementary school teacher looking to transition into an information technology job. She started with the skill of "task delegation" from her teaching job. The task associated with that skill was "assigning lesson plans to teaching assistants." The context was a school. In IT, task delegation was executed very differently, so she networked with people who worked at different companies—universities, small businesses, and big businesses—to learn how. Clearly this job switch would also involve learning a lot of new skills, but it's good to start by seeing how your keeper skills transfer to a new context first.

Person Interviewed	Job Description	Skill	Task	Context	Relevant Stressor
Thomas	Manager of an IT department at a small business	Task delegation	Organizes tickets for employee requests; delegates assignments to team	In office	It's hard to predict the flow of work. Some days have few tickets and some a lot.
Sanjay	Member of 10-person IT team at a large company	Task delegation	Directs new team members to install software on employee computers	In office	Lack of training of new employees; some need more help than others, which can eat up a lot of time

AFTER YOUR FIRST ROUND OF NETWORKING, DO AN IDENTITY CLARITY CHECK-IN

Once you have a short list of career options, I recommend doing an identity clarity check-in.

You can start with this prompt:

I would like to pursue a career in _____.
I have a number of skills that I think I can bring with me to this career, including _____ [insert keeper skill]. In my past career, I executed this skill by doing _____ [insert tasks here], but I've learned that in this career, this skill is executed by doing _____ [insert new tasks you learned about here]. I also learned that if I want to pursue this career, there are a number of new skills I will need to learn, including _____ [insert new skills here].

How hard was it to fill out this statement? You want to make sure there aren't any missing pieces before you move on to stage three.

Stage three: Go on a fact-finding mission to test whether a career is a good fit for you

Your networking journey will continue in stage three, but your goals will change. At this stage, your main goal is to dig deeper into what day-to-day life is like for a specific career. You can continue to ask people how their skills are executed at work like you did in stage two, but at this point, you want to look for consensus in people's answers, not just breadth of answers. One of my students recently started a job at a start-up, and she was shocked to find that the basic skill of "analyzing data" was executed very differently at the companies she interviewed for. Some wanted her to analyze huge data sets for many hours a day, others wanted her to do nothing but hold little workshops on how to analyze data, if they were ever able to collect any. Only by asking the same question of many people who worked in the same industry was she able to figure out how most companies would want to see her skill brought to life.

Keep in mind, too, that you can learn a lot about a profession by reading books and company websites. But your goal during stage three is to build knowledge that is *not* publicly available— norms around expectations of what it takes to get ahead; skills you need to succeed but that are rarely put in job advertisements; things like whether a potential job creates a lot of uncertainty that can be tough to manage, or very little. In other words, the "hidden curriculum." To learn it, you will need to connect with people in the positions you're interested in pursuing—a network that is narrower in scope than the one you built during stage two, when you were exploring all potential career options. These network connections, which can be more overlapping than the connections you interacted with in stage two, will help you focus on the specifics of the job. Like stage two, stage three involves asking your network questions about their jobs. But at this stage, with your new career identity starting to take form, you will want to network only with people who are in the industry you want to join.

To form this network, you can turn to the section on networking in stage two of the Drifted Apart chapter. There, I give you advice on how to identify companies you want to work for and, within these companies, people who have roles you're interested in.

LEARN THE HIDDEN CURRICULUM BY ASKING YOUR NEW CONNECTIONS TO FINISH THE SENTENCE: "BEFORE I STARTED THIS JOB, NOBODY TOLD ME THAT . . ."

It can feel embarrassing walking into a new job and realizing that you missed some key information during the interviewing or on-boarding process that everyone around you seems to know. Don't feel silly when this happens to you. It's a common experience.

In 2011, NPR ran a social experiment called "I Was Absent That Day," in which four thousand people responded to a query on Facebook to "tell us about something you were embarrassed to learn as an adult that you should have learned much earlier." One person thought the Spanish word *quesadilla* was Spanish for

"What's the deal?" Another person thought "Art Deco" was a man named Art Deco. Most people don't know the difference between a yam and a sweet potato, even chefs.

At work, we often call this knowledge the hidden curriculum—norms and expectations that aren't routinely talked about outside of the workplace but are critical for getting ahead. Sometimes the hidden curriculum reveals weird, idiosyncratic cultural norms at work. A friend of mine once poured herself a glass of orange juice from the office fridge during her first week on the job. Her colleagues looked at her in shock and horror. You can have anything from the fridge but the orange juice—that was the boss's orange juice. She had just broken a cardinal office rule. But more often, the hidden curriculum isn't about office quirks, it's about the things you ought to have accomplished or mastered but didn't—invaluable skills or experiences that a handful of lucky insiders know or have. Often, these come as unwelcome surprises.

You want to learn the hidden part of the hidden curriculum *before* you start a job, so you don't wind up drinking the proverbial orange juice. And the best way to learn it is to interact with industry insiders.

What types of things are you likely to uncover if you have your network connections go through the "Nobody told me that" exercise? To give you some insight, I ran a study in which I asked people to share their "Nobody told me that" stories, which started off a lot like the NPR experiment. I asked a group of 382 people to answer the question "Before I started this job, nobody told me that . . . ," followed by the most surprising thing they learned at work. Unadvertised responsibilities, cultural norms, hours, and pay were the largest categories of unwelcome surprises. A sizable chunk of people—20 percent—were handed different responsibilities than the ones they were told they were hired to do. Around the same percentage were shocked at weird cultural norms at work: "Nobody told me that on the first day, I was supposed to show up with candy for my team and my boss" (from someone who works in manufacturing). And perhaps not surprisingly, most of these surprises were unwelcome. Across all professions, only 5 percent of the answers were fun surprises. Nobody told me that I would get one Friday a month off, or that lunch was free (as long as you sat at your desk and ate it).

When you ask your network connections to finish the "Nobody told me that" prompt, you'll probably get answers that are as rich and varied as the ones I got. Use these answers to develop clear lines of questioning during the interview stage. If you know, for example, to probe for information about unadvertised responsibilities because many of your contacts found that they were asked to do things that the job description did not include, you can ask questions designed to detect the possibility that you'll be handed responsibilities you didn't sign up for. And as you start to see themes—answers around hours and pay, responsibilities, or general cultural norms—document them.

LEARN THE JARGON USED BY PEOPLE IN THE CAREER, AND NO, I DON'T MEAN TRENDY BUZZWORDS

In addition to learning the hidden curriculum, one goal of stage three will be to find out how much of the language used by people in a profession is completely unfamiliar to you. If your experience is anything like mine, your knowledge gap will start to emerge naturally, as you find yourself secretly googling the words people use during career conversations instead of just asking them, "What exactly do you mean by those three letters you keep stringing together?"

Jargon phrases—words or concepts used by insiders with a specific meaning that is not obvious to outsiders—are used all the time, even though many of us hate them (including scholars). Journalist Michele McGovern wrote a piece on killing jargon in the workplace, mocking phrases like "new normal," which captures something neither new nor normal.

Jargon gets a bad reputation because people use it *instead of* plain language, when plain language will do just fine. But when used appropriately, jargon allows people to say things with little effort and to convey more things in a shorter period of time. In essence, jargon allows conversations to go smoothly. New teams, for instance, will go from using everyday words that we all understand to "unusual" ones that no one outside the team understands. This insiderspeak allows them to move through ideas quickly and efficiently.

To understand the purpose jargon serves, consider how it's created. When groups work together, they start to drop function words, which are basically connective tissue in sentences (like *a*, *an*, *many*, *few*, and pronouns). They replace this connective tissue with content words that do all the work—in other words, jargon. Imagine, for example, that you're describing a test to someone. You could say, "I took a test before college that measures my aptitude for many different skills." Or you could say, "I took the ACT." "ACT" is a jargon word, and using it saves you a lot of time and effort.

The type of jargon you will need to learn is the "ACT" kind— not the "new normal" kind. "New normal" is a buzz phrase, not a useful jargon phrase. It's important to spot the difference.

How likely is it that I will encounter jargon at work?

When you've been working at one career for a long time—which is the case for many Crisis of Identity career goers—you probably use jargon regularly without realizing it. In fact, using jargon at work can signal an identity with a career, letting the world know who "belongs here" and who doesn't. Like any new language, jargon will help you communicate effectively in multiple situations, from interviews and fast-paced team conversations to Slack channel messages. And because it signals identity, using it can also help you get over the newcomer hump that many industry outsiders face when joining a new organization.

It's also something you won't be able to avoid. I asked a group of job holders the question "When you started your job, did people use words or phrases that you weren't familiar with? This can include acronyms for things (e.g., "ROI" to refer to a return on investment)." About half of people, regardless of their job title or how long they've been working, said yes (47 percent). The most common form of jargon is acronyms—shorthand words or strings of letters that stand for complex concepts—which make up about 59 percent of the jargon we encounter at work. One place where we see a lot of it is on résumés. In looking at people's résumé jargon, I found that almost all of it was acronyms: names of programs people were proficient in (Python, HTML, JavaScript) and names of certifications (USMCA Certification for someone in the automotive industry), for example.

How can I learn all this new jargon?

Jargon is everywhere. You will probably encounter new jargon every day when exploring a new career path. You'll hear it dropped casually into conversation, you'll read it in official paperwork, and you'll see it on job advertisements and people's LinkedIn profiles. You will need to understand it and use it to convey your own expertise. And because most of it will take the form of acronyms or technical terms, learning by listening is not a sufficient strategy to master it.

Try to resist the urge to nod your head in agreement when you don't understand the words people are using. Stop and ask, "Can you clarify what you mean by that?" When I was interviewing recruiters (who use a lot of acronyms) for this book, I figured out quickly that nodding was not effective. At first I tried live-googling things in the middle of calls, but it made me a terrible conversationalist. So I learned to ask.

No one made me feel silly for asking. If anything, they felt silly for assuming.

Keep in mind that most people assume that jargon is industry-wide—that it won't need to be explained to you. This bias to assume a shared understanding is one that we all have to some degree, regardless of what career we're in.

And if you feel sheepish about revealing your lack of knowledge, remind yourself how much time you will save simply by learning what these phrases mean now, rather than later. I once encountered a uniquely confusing jargon word at work—an acronym that was also a real word—while I was preparing a slide deck (another jargon term) for a talk. I was asked by a conference organizer what my preferred "WOW approach to presenting" was. Instead of asking what WOW stood for, I guessed at its meaning and spent a day trying to figure out how to dazzle my audience (Should I go for flashy slides? Wear something cool and unusual?). But WOW didn't mean dazzle, it meant "way of working." The person was asking how many prep calls I wanted.

As you encounter new jargon, create your own dictionary, like you would when learning any new language. Every time you encounter the same word, jot it down. Ask your industry connections during your chats, "What is the best way to describe my skills and accomplishments using the right insider language?" And remember as you go through the learning process, no matter how quick a learner you are, all workplaces have insiderspeak that will take some getting used to.

You will notice that as you go through the steps in stage three, your new identity will start to come into focus. Speaking like an insider (and feeling like one) will be a key part of this process. The goal during this stage is to turn over as many stones as you can so that by the end you will be ready to craft your résumé and start applying for jobs. Keep in mind that there is no hard stop to this stage; you will continue to go on a fact-finding mission during stage four, and it's natural to fine-tune your career identity as you do so. But during the interview process, the facts you discover will be less about your career in general and more about the specific role you're interested in and the organization you're thinking of working for.

Stage four: Landing the job you will love

There are two main parts to stage four: crafting your résumé and cover letters for the application process, and landing the job through the interview process. As I mentioned above, you will need to be learning skills (and getting the necessary accreditations) while going through stage three so that by the time you get to stage four, you're ready to show off those skills on your résumé (with some fancy new jargon!).

FRAMING YOUR SKILLS ON YOUR RÉSUMÉ

Before you start building your résumé, let's take stock of what you have. One, you have your list of keeper skills from stage one, along with information on how people in your future career apply these skills to their job (which you learned in stages two and three while you discovered what you want your future career to look like). Two, you have a list of new accreditations or skills you learned in parallel to networking. Three, you have a new dictionary of jargon to draw from, along with insider information on how best to use it on your résumé. And four, you have a list of any company or team outcomes you contributed to in your last career. In one of the surveys I conducted, I found that only around 21 percent of people report these contributions on their résumés (despite around 86 percent of hirers saying it "definitely helps" to do this). The Crisis of Identity career goer is often so eager to shed their old identity, they take these accomplishments off. Don't do this. These things will set you apart from the crowd. And if you've been working for a while in your old career, you probably have more of them than you realize.

With all these things in hand, you are now ready to frame your past experiences and skills in a way that will make hirers excited to bring someone like you on board.

BREAK IT DOWN, BUILD IT BACK UP

In the Drifted Apart chapter, I'll introduce the concept of "framing your skills without overselling your skills" during the application stage. This section is relevant here as well. Some Crisis of Identity career goers decide to leave their jobs for something adjacent to their current profession. If this is you, your goal is to take your basic skill set and frame it in a way that translates beyond your immediate experience. For example, imagine a woman who has been a professional wedding planner for ten years. The basic skills involved in wedding planning translate to other party planning, and a reframe would be something like, "Ten years of experience interfacing with catering company and large venues for parties with one hundred guests or more."

Other Crisis of Identity career goers decide to take a bigger leap, moving into a career that isn't adjacent to their current one. For example, imagine that the wedding planner's goal is to move beyond the party-planning industry to work in hospitality at a hotel. She will need to take a "break it down and build it back up" approach rather than a reframe.

If you're like the wedding planner turned hospitality professional, here's what you can do. First, bring in the lesson you learned in stage one of the Three Things Exercise, on how to separate your experience into task, skill, and context. The task for a wedding planner might be "getting three groups of professionals to work in sync: a catering company, a rental company that supplies chairs and tables, and a live band." The skill underlying this task is "bringing three different functions together and getting them to work efficiently toward a common goal." The context is "fancy weddings."

Second, bring in the knowledge you learned during your networking conversations on how to frame your old skill into a task that you would do in your new job. Imagine that the planner learned how the skill of "bringing different functions together"— teams of people who otherwise don't have a lot of overlap at work—is framed in the hospitality business. Perhaps in hotels that host big conferences, getting the staff at the hotel restaurant and the staff at the conference center to work together efficiently to pull off a large dinner is a rare skill, but a valued one. It takes true leadership to get these different groups in sync. The planner should focus on how she can execute her skill of bringing different functions together in the context of conference dinners at large hotels.

Third, bring in relevant jargon when describing your skill on your résumé. In hospitality, there might be different words or phrases for describing the skill of "bringing different functions together." "Function" is a jargon word, so the planner should be mindful of whether this word is used by people in hospitality.

When you describe how you contributed to team or company outcomes, you should use a combination of concrete language that describes exactly what you did in operational terms ("led a team of five that increased revenue by 20 percent, which amounted to $100,000 per quarter"), and in language that describes the contribution more broadly in terms of the skill it required ("this outcome illustrates my ability to interface between clients and team leads to improve sales numbers"). Most people do one or the other, but hirers prefer both: big-picture skills and specific, concrete outcomes.

USE JARGON SPARINGLY, AND ONLY WHEN PLAIN LANGUAGE WON'T DO

When you use jargon, be mindful that there isn't a more widely accessible alternative that would work just fine. As I recapped earlier, acronyms are common at work, but I still urge you to spell out what they mean on your résumé. Many people assume that jargon is "industry-wide," and that anyone coming across your résumé who works in that industry will understand it. But this isn't a bet I'd be willing to make. When in doubt, spell it out. Keep in mind that your jargon usage can influence the impression people have of you. Social scientist Adam Galinsky and his colleagues found that overusing jargon can backfire, creating the impression that you're doing superficial things to look like an industry insider. In fact, the more senior people become at work, the less jargon they use. The pros prefer simple, clean language.

TAILOR YOUR MATERIALS TO EACH JOB

Now that your résumé is ready, it's time to apply for jobs. A lot of people are tempted to apply for as many jobs as they can with the hopes that something will hit, especially when transitioning to a new career. In the opening to this book I came down hard on this idea, primarily because most people who do it fail to take the time to tailor their résumés to each job they apply for, and they almost never write tailor-made cover letters.

There's a formula you can follow to make cover letters for each job, starting with the Three Things Exercise to clearly illustrate what you've done in the past in a way that is very transparent to hirers. Remember, you want a good fit, and the more data you can give hirers on how you've applied your skills in the past, the better able they will be to gauge fit. Next, make it clear how those skills can transfer to the job you're applying for—a topic I covered in the last section on breaking down your skills and building them back up. Many career goers don't take this extra step. One of the best pieces of advice I've been given is "Do the work for them"—connect the dots for the reader between your old experiences and skills and the new ones you're looking to undertake. Don't assume that they are motivated, or even have the time, to do this themselves.

For example, our wedding planner can write in a cover letter:

"In my past career, I brought different functions together in the wedding planning business. I regularly worked with multiple vendors—catering staff, musicians, and florists, for example—to streamline a flow of work to execute large events, often under tight time frames. In hospitality, I would love to apply this skill in the context of large conferences. My experience working with many vendors makes me well suited to the job of bringing restaurant staff and conference organizers together."

THE INTERVIEW

Most people think of the interview as a chance to impress hirers. The goal, of course, is to land the job. Think of the interview as a two-way street—you're interviewing them as much as they're interviewing you. There are times during an interview when you need to play detective, something I will get to shortly. But first, let's focus on how you can impress the interviewer.

Communicate that you have a clear career identity

One of the first things you need to do thoughtfully throughout this process is clearly communicate what your new identity is. In stage one I gave you the tools you need to find clarity around your new identity before you start interviewing. Communicating this clarity, it turns out, is equally important.

I spoke with Sima Vaisman, an executive recruiter with a specialty in IT health care and informatics, who reminded me that despite trends in hiring, there has always been one thing that makes companies nervous: hiring someone who lacks clarity around who they are and where they want to go. Hirers have a safety bias—they want to know exactly what they're getting out of a candidate and what their developmental trajectory will look like over the next few years.

"It is very common to see hiring managers terrified of making hiring mistakes," Sima told me. "They usually try to hire the 'safe résumé,' not necessarily the best person"—in essence, the person who looks like every other successful person hired into this role before them. Same background, same trajectory, same prior roles. Much of this fear stems from impression management concerns, especially among top companies with solid reputations. Companies hire safely for the same reason that despite there being five new restaurants in town, you eat at the same one every time. Most people prefer predictability over adventure. If you enter the job market with the mindset that you're managing an organization's fear of uncertainty, you can act more strategically to create that certainty during the interview.

To get started, pull up the paragraph describing your new identity that you completed at the identity check-in in stage two. This paragraph can help you draft a script of how you will talk about yourself (and yes, some scripting is necessary, even during casual interview conversations). If you need some inspiration, borrow from the clear identity example from the Dobrow and Higgins study. Statements that subtly convey confidence, such as "My professional history clearly points in the direction of . . . ," can ease a hiring manager's concerns that you're not ready to make a big change. Avoid language that signals ambiguity about what direction you want to go in, like "I might want to be a manager, but I also might just want to be an individual contributor to start off." These two things—manager and individual contributor—are such distinct roles that you should know which of them you want before you start applying for jobs. In my field of social psychology, one of the biggest mistakes that prospective graduate students make during interviews is telling me that they've applied for PhD programs in social psychology *and* clinical psychology. This might seem like a subtle distinction, but for a scholar it's a huge one: they are radically different fields and have different career trajectories. If you don't know which direction you want to go in during the interview, you're not ready to commit to a PhD program. At the very least, don't show that ambivalence to the prospective interviewer!

As you work on your script, keep in mind that admitting areas for growth is a good thing. Don't confuse identity clarity with overselling yourself. Hirers look for people who both know what they want to do next and are clear on what on-the-job training they will need to get there successfully.

Work on your story of how you got from "there" to "here"

Most of us meander in our careers; it's rare to find someone who knew what they wanted to do at a young age and stuck with it. But this doesn't stop interviewers from wanting to hear a cohesive story of how you got from "there" to "here."

I remember my first attempt at telling my story when applying for faculty positions out of graduate school. The academic job statement is a narrative about your research, and it's supposed to read like a short story, with a plot, a protagonist (the writer), and a handful of other characters (collaborators and mentors). But the problem was, I spent a good two years running a series of failed studies—most of them on lie detection—that did little to advance the plot. Unfortunately, I wasn't yet at the career stage where I could leave this stuff out; I had only so many publications to showcase. My decision to run these studies needed to seem intentional, or at least have some teachable moments.

It wasn't easy. And honestly, this skill still doesn't come naturally to me.

But I learned that finding a thread of similarity between yesterday's experience and today's is key to making a meandering journey feel deliberate. For me, this meant finding something about my lie detection studies that inspired my next career move. It wasn't the findings from these studies or even the topic that moved the plot along; it was the methodology. My failed foray into the science of lie detection was the first time I designed a real social interaction study in the lab; it kick-started my identity as a scientist who studies the uncomfortable, anxiety-inducing moments of everyday life.

Many of the hirers I interviewed were career transitioners themselves, and they know the value of this skill. Take, for example, Ethan Mao, who was a lobster fisherperson before turning to recruiting. When I asked Ethan to describe his journey, he didn't just talk about the moves he made, he also talked about how he transferred skills in ways that were novel and interesting. Ethan left the fishing business because of research he did in college predicting a shortage of (literal) lobsters in the Gulf of Maine. And he got into recruiting because his girlfriend at the time was doing recruiting. But here's his version:

"At a young age, I was both employed by large commercial captains while also employing other folks like myself for my own lobstering operations. As a result, I felt comfortable growing both as an individual contributor and leader, and working with clients and candidates alike." Ethan realized that his ability to work for large commercial captains in the fishing industry while also employing other lobster fisherfolk was a lot like liaising between a corporation doing hiring and job candidates who want to work for those corporations.

And there you have it. A connection between two careers that on the surface have nothing to do with each other.

What questions should I ask during the interview?

With the "Nobody told me that" data, I gave you a taste of what surprises you might encounter at work when the norms and expectations of a workplace aren't made explicit. Many of the questions I recommend you ask are geared toward uncovering these potential surprises.

During the interview process, you want to look for signs that a workplace makes an effort to reduce the knowledge gap between those who know the hidden curriculum and those who don't.

Transitioners, even those who've been experts in another profession, need a lot of guardrails in place when they start: procedures for big things, like how performance reviews are done, and small things, like what's a reasonable amount of time in advance to request a meeting with a boss. Handbooks and resources that spell out what each person's role entails are critical. So, too, are signs that a workplace makes an effort to provide network connections to those who don't already have those connections in place, like insiders do (remember, three quarters of people's connections come from their organization or industry). My favorite example of this is the "have it" (where people post the skills or resources they have) and "want it" (where people post the skills or resources they need) board at work; it can make it easy for people to find one another. Keep in mind, too, that at work, knowledge is often transferred via word of mouth, but if you're a career transitioner, you will need a much more concrete and reliable method of learning new things.

Critical questions

Here are some critical questions, which I will return to in other chapters in the book. They are good questions to reflect on for all interviews, no matter what type of career goer you identify with most strongly. After these top five questions, I provide more specific ones for the Crisis of Identity career goer.

What is the goal of the interview?
Most interviewers will give you some details about what will be asked in anticipation of the actual interview, if you ask. For exam-

ple, internal recruiter Meghan Conaty tells people that during the interview they will walk through a business case, and she gives them a one-pager on how they will be scored. The "no-surprises" approach to interviewing allows candidates to prepare so they show up as the best version of themselves, not the most anxious. The willingness of an interviewer to give you questions ahead of time is a good sign that the company doesn't believe in "gotcha!" moments, intentionally catching candidates off guard. And if you get a hard no? See this as a warning sign. The company might not know what the structure of the interview will be yet, which can happen when a job description is posted before a role is clearly defined.

In other cases, the process is organized enough to guarantee that a standard set of questions is asked of everyone, but not enough to figure out who's doing the asking. Ethan Mao reminded me that it's not uncommon to show up to a third- or fourth-stage interview only to learn very quickly that the questions being asked of you have been asked already. Sometimes, the company does this because they are looking for consistency in answers. But the interview shouldn't feel like Groundhog Day. There should be a good answer to the question "Is there a reason why I'm being asked these questions again?"

How did the job come to be?

If you ask your first point of contact (and your second and third) this question, you will soon learn that "How did the job come to be?" can have many answers. The hiring experts I spoke with recommend collecting answers to this question from all the people you interview with, because a lack of consensus among interviewers can signal that the role is not clearly defined. One leader I spoke with created a new role of personal assistant for her job. She created the position for herself, but several other leaders (who also wanted a personal assistant) thought it was for them. In the end, the newly hired personal assistant lasted two weeks. It's a shame she didn't ask, "How did this job come to be?" of all the people who interviewed her. Every single person would have answered, "Because I need a new personal assistant!"

You might also want to ask as a follow-up, "Was the job posted more than once?" Job advertisements are often taken down and put back up for a variety of reasons, ranging from changing needs to "We didn't find anyone, so we decided to cast a wider net this time." This simple question can help you understand the internal dynamics at the organization.

How much have you interfaced with the hiring manager?

This question is specific to interviews with a recruiter. Career transition coach Erin Andersen recommends gaining clarity on how much shared reality there is among the people involved in hiring, given that your future boss might be far removed from the interview process. "The biggest issue with the recruiter is that they don't work in the department themselves, and they therefore really don't understand the role," she told me. Ask the hiring manager, "How much have you interfaced with my future boss?" The further your boss is from the people interviewing you, the stronger the likelihood that what is promised to you won't be delivered.

For some jobs, the person who wrote the ad is so high up it's not practical to interface with them during the interview—say, the CEO. Ethan Mao suggests you ask to meet with multiple people in the interview process (including a team member of the team you would eventually join). People in parallel roles can give you an understanding of what the day-to-day looks like. Which leads to my next question.

Can you please provide me with a sense of what the day-to-day of this job will look like?

Most hirers I spoke with recommend asking this question once you've moved far along in the interview process (the third or fourth round). That's the stage when things start to get much more concrete. Keep in mind your results from the Daily Stress Test I introduced you to in the opening, looking out for the things that triggered your stress in the past (like having meetings removed from your calendar thirty minutes before the meeting). Knowledge of these triggers, along with your must-have list, can guide you to ask the right questions when looking for fit.

William Tincup used the day-in-the-life technique when he owned an ad agency to make sure job candidates had a realistic perspective on what the job would look like. "I wouldn't hire anybody until they came and worked with us for a day," he told me. "Not [to do] work, but to learn the day-to-day with no pomp and circumstance." The key here is the "no pomp and circumstance." How loud is the office? How many people show up? How fast-paced are things, and do senior leaders yell at people or handle them with care? These things can be gleaned by the environment.

Can I interview at the office (if there is one)?

Lately there's been a lot of discussion about where we should be holding interviews, especially for hybrid or in-office jobs. Most experts I spoke with agreed that in-office is preferable, especially if that's where you will work.

"If you look at where the interview is held—whether it's in a small meeting room or conference room—it's typical for it to be strategically placed at the front of the office. The candidate isn't automatically walking through the entire office to get to the interview," Erin Andersen told me. In her experience, setups like this one are a good indication that the rest of the office isn't prepped, and if you ask for a tour of the office, you're likely to see people in their natural habitat. Once you've seen the office, ask yourself, "Do people look happy? Are they diverse? Are people engaged in their work? If it's lunch hour, are people still at their desk, or do they take their break?" Erin goes as far as recommending that people request a lunchtime interview to get at this last question.

Erin's approach to learning about an office environment is grounded in social science research on measuring personalities of people based on their living environments. Small things, like where people sit, how close the executives are to everyone else, and the state of the in-office kitchen (has it been used in the last six months?), can tell us a lot about an office vibe.

▪ ▪ ▪

Questions for Crisis of Identity career goers

In addition to the five critical questions, there are some important ones you should ask if you're going through an identity crisis.

How much direct experience on the job is necessary for performing well here?

I've spent much of this chapter teaching you how to frame your skills in a way that will make them appealing to hirers. But in some professions, there's no way around the need for direct experience. This point came across loud and clear in the "Nobody told me that" exercise, in which many of the unwanted surprises referred to additional responsibilities at work, including tasks that only direct experience would help the new hire prepare for (like lifting heavy furniture when working in an art warehouse). Direct experience often exposes people to the less-advertised side of the career. But it has an added benefit beyond learning new skills—it helps you form social connections.

New York City hair stylist Joshua Barbieri apprenticed for Vidal Sassoon in San Francisco in the 1990s for his direct experience out of finishing school. During that time he was cajoled into doing things like giving a woman with gorgeous long blond hair a "grandma cut," so he learned how to handle unhappy clients (and sadistic bosses, apparently). It wasn't the hands-on experience that really mattered for Josh, it was the social connections that came out of it. Working at Vidal Sassoon was almost like a key that opened an invisible door to the profession. With it, Josh was able to build an enviable client list through recommendations that came straight from Vidal Sassoon. Prior experience was necessary to setting up a practice in this profession. Dentists, perhaps surprisingly, operate in a similar way. Those who start their own practices often piggyback on a more established dentist, sharing their office and their patients. Many buy the senior dentist's patient list when that dentist is ready to retire so they don't have to build their own. Direct experience working with a more advanced dentist really amounts to buying a black book of names.

Is there hands-on training for people like me?

One of the biggest reasons why Crisis of Identity career goers fail to transition successfully into a new industry isn't because they don't have transferable skills, it's because there's no scaffolding in place to help them transfer those skills to a new environment. Learning doesn't happen magically through osmosis, nor does it happen simply by hanging around smart people who are good at their jobs. It happens when organizations put concrete steps in place to make sure their employees don't have long "Nobody told me that" lists. And one way to do that is through training.

During the interview, ask whether the organization has formal training for transitioners like you. For example, if you work in sales or marketing, can you see what a successful version of a client pitch looks like—and what an unsuccessful one looks like? Is there someone who can train you to make sure your pitches look like the former? Will you be coached on negotiating prices with clients, and on upselling (jargon for getting people to buy more than they bargained for)?

Resources like these not only help you learn, they also cut down on the number of help-request emails you will need to send out when you're getting started. Most of us know the feeling of power-lessness when you can't take the next step until somebody writes us back. Learning from others is a good thing, but being completely dependent on them to do the basic elements of your job is not.

During the interview, also ask about the feedback structure. If you've read my book *Jerks at Work* you know that I'm a big fan of feedback that is frequent and specific. For newcomers, this type of feedback is critical. Part of your learning process will be getting this feedback, and the person interviewing you should be able to tell you what to expect the feedback structure to be.

Last, ask if there's a window of time dedicated to learning. I don't mean a three-month window in which no one is evaluating the quality of your work because it's your "learning period," I mean a time in which you can get the hands-on direct experience you need. Questions like "Will I be able to shadow another employee who's an expert at my role?" and "Will I receive timely feedback on my progress?" are reasonable asks.

What are the most common reasons why transitioners like me have failed at this job before?

I'm a big fan of asking interviewers what it looks like when people fail. This might seem a bit negative (why not ask what it looks like when people succeed?), but the reason is simple. When people crash and burn, hirers usually have a good idea why. Hindsight is twenty-twenty, and losses loom larger than gains. Hirers remember the mistakes they made at the hiring stage—what skills they missed and what they didn't have the foresight to anticipate—that led to the eventual failure of a hire.

Janet, a company president, realized early on that one of the main reasons why Crisis of Identity transitioners failed in the consulting business was because even though they had a wealth of knowledge about the products they were selling (and many had PhDs in psychology, which made them great assets to the research and development department), they had little direct experience with clients. These transitioners, who often came from jobs in lab research, had a hard time setting boundaries with clients. Many got themselves into tough spots by overpromising things they couldn't deliver. After a few hiring mistakes, Janet developed a new rule: No matter how knowledgeable someone was about the content, she could not hire them until they had worked directly with clients. She had to overcome this barrier herself as a career transitioner, working for a few months with a consulting firm where she was a fly on the wall during client calls before they let her speak up.

The person interviewing you should be able to answer the question "Why did the last person fail?" with specific behavioral examples. If they answer with vague platitudes like "They just weren't what we were looking for," then there's a good chance they don't have traction on the "why they failed" piece. You want to work in an environment where your supervisor and your team understand your entry point as a transitioner, know the possible ways in which you could fail at this job, and are preemptive about putting steps in place to prevent that failure.

▪ ▪

TAKE-HOMES FOR EACH STAGE

STAGE ONE:

- Understand how strongly you still identify with your old career, measuring it multiple times and looking for consistency before you move to the next stage.

- Use your answers from the Daily Stress Test to get insight into what causes your feelings about your career identity to go up and down.

STAGE TWO:

- List your current skills using the Three Things Exercise: What is a task you do at work, what is the skill it takes to execute that task, and what is the context in which you do it?

- Build a network of people who have different experiences, work in different companies, and have different job titles. In other words, people with nonoverlapping information.

STAGE THREE:

- Continue your networking and career conversations, focusing on people who work in the same industry but in different companies, so you can take a deep dive into what the day-to-day looks like at your future job.

- Learn the hidden curriculum—rules and norms that aren't publicized on company websites—and new jargon.

STAGE FOUR:

▪ Create tailored résumés and cover letters for each job you apply for, making it clear how your current skills transfer to your new profession. Treat the interview like a two-way street. Ask questions that give insight into hidden norms at work, including skills and experiences you're expected to have that aren't advertised but are expected of you.

THE DRIFTED APART

I used to love my job,
but I no longer recognize it

I can't believe I used to do this damn commute every day."

Mia, a marketing expert, is having a hard time with this whole you-must-come-back-in-person business. We're two years post-pandemic, and still, coming into the city on her compulsory "in" days makes about as much sense to Mia as wearing a school uniform did in middle school. It feels forced and restrictive, and has zero impact on her ability to get work done.

Most of us can relate to Mia's frustration; no one likes to be told they must come back to the office, especially if the experience offers little more than a change of scenery. But this conversation is catching me a little off guard. Mia used to *love* coming to work. She was so miserable with having her social interactions reduced to small squares on a screen, I thought she would be one of the first people to want back in.

"In my defense, it doesn't help that we don't really have an office anymore. We're doing this thing called 'hoteling,' where we basically meet in a different hotel conference room on our 'in' days," she tells me. Lots of companies don't want to make huge rents, so they've started renting out rooms in various locations, hotels included.

When I press her on whether the faux office is the problem, she hedges a bit. "Maybe, but I don't know, lots of things have changed," she says. The source of Mia's unhappiness seems nebulous, tough to pin down. There doesn't seem to be one (or even two or three) specific things wrong, it's the whole vibe at work that's changed. People seem less engaged and less willing to help one another out. They walk around the "office" like bored zombies, and no one cares if they close a deal or not. To Mia, it's like living in a world that was once painted in color but is now in muted tones.

For the Drifted Apart like Mia, the biggest challenge is pinning down what exactly is wrong, or what has changed with the job. Mia has a list of contenders. First there were pandemic-related budget cuts, and people lost the creature comforts that made the office cozy. Then the economy tanked. Some people were laid off, and the ones who stuck around had their bonuses cut. But even worse, the leftovers, like Mia, felt underworked and underutilized. And now, following restructuring, Mia's job is a combination of her old job along with other people's jobs that she now has the bandwidth to do, but not the expertise.

The whole thing sounds like a giant mess.

I ask Mia what would need to change for the company to get its groove back, but she honestly has no idea. It's quite possible that during the last few years Mia's interests have changed, too, that "winning big contracts" no longer does it for her, but she's not sure. Like many Drifted Apart, Mia remembers what used to make her happy at work and knows this isn't it, but she has no idea how to fix it. And importantly, she keeps trying to connect the dots between big changes at work—layoffs, budget cuts, and restructures—and the little ones that affect her day-to-day job—disengaged colleagues and meetings full of milquetoast ideas. But seeing patterns in these changes is a challenge, and one that most of us would struggle with.

What is a Drifted Apart career goer?

This chapter is for the person who thinks they know what they want out of a job, and at one point might have had it. But now they feel disengaged at work, bitter even, that so much has changed around them. They no longer recognize the job they have, and they worry about who they might become if they stick around much longer.

Psychologically, drifting apart from a job is similar to drifting apart from a romantic partner. At one point you couldn't imagine being away from this person. Conversations went on for hours, and everything just clicked. But instead of sitting through awkward date nights wondering why you once found this person so charming, you're sitting through meetings with customers or colleagues feigning enthusiasm for the "new initiative" you're working on together. As you go through the motions, you ask yourself, "When was the turning point in this relationship, and who's to blame?"

But like most relationships that fizzle, the change of heart probably didn't happen overnight. Rather, it was a series of small things, adding up over time, that slowly ate away at the meaning you derive from your work. Understanding how your path to unhappiness unfolded will be critical for stage two: figuring out what you want your future career to look like. And to do that, you'll need to play detective and do a little digging to apprehend how different types of changes that occurred at work are related to one another—from big ones, like changes in work-from-home policies, to daily ones, like how many hours you typically have to finish something.

When we feel ourselves drifting apart from our jobs, the first step we usually take is to create a list of the things that we're unhappy with so that when we job hunt, we know what to look out for. Often this list includes comparisons between the past and the present. "I used to have two weeks to turn around a new report and now I have two days," or "I used to work with a solid team of five, but after the layoffs, they were all replaced with new people who have no experience. I can't even remember their names!"

The Drifted Apart often focus on what they've lost. This is true across all relationships, and the one with your job is no exception.

I recommend a different strategy. I urge you to first take a step back and think about the changes to the workplace you have experienced, good and bad—things like who sits next to you at work, who your boss is, and whether there was a new software system that everyone was expected to learn, but only a few actually did. These are the changes that you see and feel.

Next, think about the changes that are hidden from view—big

and structural, beyond your control, and often out of your line of sight. Focus on organizational-level changes, like changes to the leadership team, to the work-from-home policies, and to the budget.

We often don't see the connection between these two types of changes, but like a puppet master pulling on strings, these top-down changes shape everything about your job, from how likely it is that you will get a raise this year, to the ever-changing demands that your boss places on you. As you move through stages two and three, you will want to ask your network connections to explain not only *whether* an organizational change like budget cuts influenced things like the makeup of people's teams, but also *how* they influenced them.

In the last part of your discovery journey, I show you how to measure the ways in which you've changed along the way. In all types of relationships that involve drifting apart, it's much easier to see how changes in the other person, or in this case, the workplace, have contributed to relationship decay. But it's almost always the case that both parties have changed. I will help you explore how you've grown since you started feeling disconnected, from how your goals and motivations have changed, to where you find meaning at work. I also urge you to focus on lateral changes you've experienced—we don't always become better or worse over time, but different.

At the end of this section, your goal will be to put all these pieces together to create a story of how you got to this place. You might not be able to control the big structural changes to your job that lead you to feel disconnected, but you will have a sense of what changes contributed to them. This will help you ask the right questions during the next stages of career discovery to be sure there's no misalignment between what is promised to you during the interview and what the job will deliver. Miscommunications arise frequently during the interview and onboarding processes. For the Drifted Apart, detecting these small miscommunications along the way will reduce the likelihood of drifting apart in a new position.

Stage one: Why am I unhappy here?

Imagine, like Mia, that you've noticed several changes to the workplace, from layoffs to a reorganization, that all seem to affect how you work and who you work with. When it comes to explaining her unhappiness, Mia had an instinct to "think big" with her list of causes, focusing on organizational-level changes like layoffs and budget cuts. I urge you instead to first "think small," focusing on the changes that directly impacted you.

> **What changes have I experienced to my job?**

On the next page is a list of twelve common changes to the workplace, all of which can trigger unwelcome psychological changes, including increasing uncertainty and reducing autonomy and psychological safety. Which of these changes have occurred since you started feeling Drifted Apart?

Check all that apply:

CHANGES TO MY JOB

☐ The people on my team
☐ The amount of things I'm responsible for at one time
☐ My job duties
☐ Who I report to (boss or team leader)
☐ Who I work physically close to (even if not directly with)
☐ The pace at which I'm expected to get things done
☐ My work hours
☐ Who I informally interact with at work (have coffee with, chat in the hall with)
☐ The number of people my boss or supervisor is responsible for overseeing
☐ How often I meet with my supervisor or boss
☐ The number of people I'm responsible for overseeing
☐ How much I travel

How many changes did you check off?

When I asked two hundred people who used to love their jobs to do the same thing, I found that the most common changes are ones related to whom we work with—bosses, leaders, teammates, and the people we are physically close to—and changes in job responsibilities and tasks. The most frequent changes were:

1. The people on my team (81 percent)

2. The amount of things I'm responsible for at one time (69 percent)

3. My job duties (67 percent)

4. Who I report to (boss or team leader) (58 percent)

5. Who I work physically close to (even if not directly with) (57 percent)

People feel drifted apart from their jobs because their relationships at work have changed. Many people have also seen a shift from what they were hired to do to what they're doing now.

> **Are there organizational changes that happened at the top that trickled down to affect the changes I experienced?**

Now that you have your list of the small changes you've felt, you can start to think big: Are there big organizational-level changes that explain the changes you've experienced? Perhaps, like Mia, you experienced a restructuring that shifted the makeup of teams, which in turn impacted the jobs you were asked to do. I just made a causal association between these two things, but in reality, connecting the dots between these big workplace changes and the daily ones you feel is no easy feat. Few of us have a bird's-eye view at work; we don't see how decisions made behind closed doors trickle down to affect us.

To help close that information gap, I went right to the source and surveyed 150 decision-makers across dozens of professions who worked behind the scenes to orchestrate and roll out changes to the workplace.

I presented these leaders with the same list of twelve workplace changes that people experience along with a list of ten organizational-level changes, and I had them play a matching game between the two. They could draw as many associations as they wanted between an organizational-level change and a change people felt in their everyday work. Here's the list of organizational changes.

ORGANIZATIONAL-LEVEL CHANGES

- ☐ How bonuses, raises, and salaries are structured
- ☐ Team reorganization (e.g., two teams become one)
- ☐ Change in work-from-home policies
- ☐ New CEO or senior leader who oversees things
- ☐ Layoffs
- ☐ New software system that affects how people work
- ☐ Move to a different office
- ☐ Layout of the office
- ☐ Merger between your company and another
- ☐ The global economy

Interestingly, I found that only 16 percent of leaders associated one of the top five changes experienced by the Drifted Apart with an organizational-level change. This number is pretty small, considering that 50 percent of leaders in the study said they felt both types of changes. Even the people who helped plan or roll out big changes and witnessed daily changes to people's work lives are largely at a loss when it comes to understanding how one change *caused* another.

It's very easy for us to draw conclusions about how big-picture changes trickle down to affect us. We say things like "After layoffs and budget cuts, the people on my team all changed, so I want to avoid working for a place that might be doing layoffs and budget cuts in the future." But as these data show, even the people in charge of layoffs and budget cuts don't see such clear connections. We simply cannot assume that these associations exist in the real world as clearly as they might in our heads. In stages two and three, if a network connection makes a comment like this, ask them *how* the changes are associated, not just *whether* they are. You want to see evidence that the connection is indeed real.

Last, make sure you probe for changes that are unexpected or off the radar. I was surprised to see "a new software system" show up twice among the top five change associations for leaders. When it comes to explaining why we're unhappy at work, we often focus on changes that everyone is talking about—layoffs, budget cuts, and the global economy are the big contenders. But often it's the ones that sneak up on us and influence our work in unforeseen ways. To detect these types of changes, ask your network connections, "Did you notice any surprising or unexpected changes to the organization lately [like software system changes]?" You want to get people to think outside the box to uncover these hidden contenders.

How have I changed since I started working here?

Now that you have some data on the types of changes that have happened to the workplace, it's time to shift gears and think about you. Up to this point, I've been focusing on how workplace changes are the likely culprit behind feeling disconnected from your job. But you've probably changed, too, in ways that can be difficult to detect. Slowly, over time, many of us shift our values, goals, and even personality traits, without realizing it.

In fact, personality psychologist Nathan Hudson and his colleagues found that changes to core personality traits are often undetectable. At the start of a sixteen-week longitudinal study, they had people rate themselves on the "Big Five" personality traits (extraversion, agreeableness, conscientiousness, emotional stability, and openness to experience). These traits are not only central to people's sense of self but also strong predictors of behavior across social situations. Then, every four weeks, they rated themselves again on the Big Five, and how much the study participants thought their personality changed in the last month.

What did they find?

Most people were moderately accurate in knowing how much they rated their personalities as changing over the course of the study (around 60 percent were in the ballpark of knowing the direction of change and how much they changed, if there was a change). But when they were wrong, they were really wrong. Across the five personality traits, nearly 40 percent of people perceived change in the opposite direction from what they had reported. People simply didn't keep track of how they rated their own changes over time. For example, 25 percent of people thought they had become more extraverted over time, but in reality, they reported a decrease in extraversion over the course of the study. Another 10 percent of people thought they had become less extraverted, when in reality they reported becoming more extraverted.

So what lessons can the Drifted Apart take from this study?

Our confidence in how we've changed isn't necessarily related to how much we've actually changed. And we clearly aren't great at keeping track of our own self-reported changes over time. Maybe you think you haven't changed at all—that it's only the job that's changed. Or maybe you think you've changed a lot, probably in a positive direction—getting wiser, more responsible, or more skilled. As Nathan Hudson's study found, we make mistakes in both directions, but the most common ones are the ones that paint us in a positive light.

I've routinely found myself saying things like, "I am definitely not as lazy as I was in 2019! I spent a lot of time watching streaming that year." Truth be told, I'm probably lazier now, with the streaming hours to prove it. But my desire to derogate my past lazy self makes sense. Most of us want to improve over time. Nathan Hudson and his colleagues saw this pattern in their data—most people made self-enhancing errors. The Drifted Apart in my study also showed this bias. I asked people how much they thought they'd outgrown their job and how much they thought the job had outgrown them. Using a scale of 1 to 5 for these two questions, most people are about 1.5 points apart, in the direction of thinking that they've outgrown the job more than the job has outgrown them. We get better, our jobs get worse.

The second mistake we make is that we think too abstractly about change, which can obscure the specific ways in which we've changed. I asked half of the Drifted Apart in my study to fill out the sentence "I used to be _____ and now I'm _____," following this prompt: "We are interested in the ways in which you think you've changed since you've noticed changes to the job." I gave them five of these sentences to fill out.

Most people focused on emotions—I used to be happy and now I'm tired. I used to be interested and now I'm bored. Focusing on how we felt in the past compared to now is natural, but it's not useful for a job hunt. You want to list concrete things that you would like to see in your next job.

To help people get more concrete, the other half of the Drifted Apart were given this prompt: "I used to *prefer* X, and now I *prefer* Y." These answers got at the root of people's needs.

- I used to prefer in-person meetings and now I prefer virtual ones.

- I used to prefer working alone and now I prefer an open office.

One finding that surprised me was the number of lateral comparisons people made: ways in which they didn't necessarily get better or worse, just different. Lateral changes happen frequently in our lives; we start to prefer tea over coffee, earlier bedtimes instead of later ones. We grow laterally at work, too, but we often don't realize it. Perhaps you used to prefer an open office environment, and now you prefer to work from home.

So when it comes to thinking about what you want next, make sure you start with the statement "I used to prefer X and now I prefer Y." Avoid the general one: "I used to be X and now I am Y." That prompt will lead you astray.

Have a go:

I used to prefer _____ and now I prefer _____ .

CREATE A LIST OF PREFERENCES

In stage one, I've asked you to think about a lot of moving parts. How should you organize what you learned in a way that will be the most useful for stage two? Your goal is to create a list of preferences, written out in concrete terms, for your future job search. To create this list, draw from the preferences exercise ("I used to prefer X, and now I prefer Y"), bringing in insights from the Changes to My Job checklist that are the most relevant to that specific preference. For example, imagine that you noticed an unwelcome change to meetings with your boss—they used to be consistent and weekly, and now they're sporadic. You also noted during the preferences exercise that you used to prefer autonomy at work (being left alone), but now that you're on a clear leadership path, you really want to work for a boss with a scheduled feedback plan. These two things—a consistent meeting schedule and a clear feedback structure—go hand in hand.

Once you have your list, order your preferences by rank so that you end up with a list with three categories: must-haves, things it would be nice to have, and things you're willing to cave on. These three categories might shift around a bit during stage two, but your goal is to have a starting point.

Stage two: What do I want my future career to look like?

In many ways, the Drifted Apart are one the luckier groups of job seekers I cover in this book. They know what a good relationship with a job feels like; the difficulty lies in figuring out what they need to do to reproduce it. To that end, I've organized stage two around three main questions that the Drifted Apart will need to answer:

1. Do I have a good sense of how quickly my industry is changing, not just my job?

2. If yes, are the changes to my industry so drastic that I might want to consider a career change?

3. If I do want to stay in this career, how likely is it that I will find all my must-haves in one place?

I elaborate on each question below, and then I provide a networking guide to help you answer them. Like the Crisis of Identity career transitioner, the Drifted Apart career goer will learn a specific networking strategy designed to address their specific needs.

Do I have a good sense of how quickly my industry is changing?

It might be the case that you've not simply drifted apart from your job, you've drifted apart from your entire career. Many of us feel like our industries have changed so radically in recent years that we've been thrown into an era of chaos. But not all careers are changing at the same pace—some have stayed surprisingly stable, whereas some have undergone massive evolutions.

If you're unsure of whether your current career is changing at a quick clip, you can start by digging into the "future of work" world to get a sense of big-picture changes. For example, the U.S. Bureau of Labor Statistics reports changes on dimensions like job growth rate, compensation, and skills that are required to enter a career. McKinsey & Company provides a breakdown of which careers are static (including jobs that involve communication, like consultants), declining (jobs that involve collecting and processing data, like accounting and paralegal work), and evolving (jobs that involve health care, like medicine and nursing).

In the chapter on the Crisis of Identity career goer, I talked about discovering the hidden curriculum at work by asking people to finish the sentence "Before I started this job, nobody told me that . . ." with the goal of leaving no stone unturned when you're venturing into unfamiliar career territory. The Drifted Apart also need to discover hidden information, but specific to *changes* in people's jobs. During networking conversations with people who hold jobs similar to the ones you want, ask your connections, "What are some changes to your career you've experienced in the last few years that people aren't really talking about? What have the new people who've come on board been surprised at?"

Your goal during these conversations is to capture trends that aren't well documented, those that are under the radar and haven't yet made it to a global jobs report. When you ask this question, think small. People are pretty good at recalling changes to their daily work lives that either threw a wrench into things or made their lives surprisingly better. I learned this lesson during a recent hospital stay. Over the course of my visit, the most consistent topic of conversation among the nursing staff was the hospital's new parking policy (they used to be able to park in the patient lot, but now they had to park in an adjacent lot that was farther away). Lunch breaks (which are short) outside the hospital were now impossible, and people had to spend an extra twenty minutes a day getting to work. Clearly this small change, likely orchestrated by someone at the top for reasons unknown, had a huge impact on people's workdays. A few more unwelcome changes like this, and half those nurses will be Drifted Apart in a year's time.

Has my career moved in an entirely new direction?

As you start to network with people in your career, themes around the nature of changes will begin to emerge. Some changes are so radical you might wonder if your career has moved in an entirely new direction (and one that you're not comfortable with). One of the best ways you can detect this type of change is by asking your connections to talk about changes in their daily tasks: "Have the tasks you're doing changed so much that your job has become unrecognizable from the one you once had?" If you get a lot of yeses, you might be part of a bigger industry-wide change.

I spoke with Tricia Baker, a school psychologist turned therapist who is among this crowd. "When I first started as a school psychologist, I was working one-on-one with teens who really needed help. They had major problems at home; many had a history of abuse. I felt like I was really making a difference. But then my job changed. I spent all day testing kids for Individualized Education Programs (IEPs). I gave a test, I scored it, and I wrote up a report. Testing kids is part of a school psychologist's job, but it shouldn't be the whole job. And it wasn't the job I signed up for."

Tricia eventually realized that it wasn't just her job as a school psychologist that had changed, it was the career of a school psychologist. Being able to administer and efficiently score tests for students was more valued than helping them resolve conflicts and handle emotional issues, at least in the schools in the district she was willing to work in. She learned this by networking with other school psychologists. For Tricia, realizing that she needed a career change, not just a job change, was an important part of her journey. She went back to school, got a master's degree in clinical psychology, and started her transition. It turns out that the Crisis of Identity chapter was more relevant to her than this one, and it might be to you too.

If, however, you learn that the changes to your career aren't so drastic that you want out, then you will need to return to your preferences list. At this point, you've done enough digging to confidently tell yourself, "This is the career I want to stick with." The advice I give in the remainder of this chapter is for the person who has decided to stay in their industry but wants to work for a different company.

How should I network to answer these stage-two questions?

As I mentioned in the opening and the Crisis of Identity chapter, there's no better way to learn about a career than to talk to people. But when it comes to forming new networking connections, there's no one right or wrong way to do it. I elaborate on whom to network with, but remember as you go through this process that networking doesn't need to feel "schmoozy," where you're only talking to these people to promote yourself. Your goal is to uncover hidden knowledge that people aren't frequently talking about; daily experiences, like how far they need to park to get to the office, that impact their work lives.

First, identify the organizations you want to work in, then reach out to people who hire

What is the best strategy for networking for the Drifted Apart? Assuming that you've decided to stick with your current career (you're not a Crisis of Identity career goer), you want to first identify potential organizations or companies that you might want to work with in the future.

Why not start with talking to people who have your dream job, regardless of where they work? During stage two, your main goal is to understand the relationship between your preferences (and whether a place you're considering has them) and what changes at work might influence the degree to which those preferences will still exist in the future. Often changes experienced at work affect multiple people—they cut across roles, teams, and managers. The Changes to My Job checklist, for example, included changes to who is on your team, but even this "local" change likely affects many people at the organization, no matter what team they're on. It was certainly the case that in the hospital where I stayed it wasn't just the nurses who were affected by the parking lot change; the physicians and the cleaning staff complained too. The more people you talk to who work for an organization, the better your understanding will be of how widespread certain changes are and, in turn, the likelihood that a future change would affect you. People might not understand the source of changes—and as I illustrated in stage one, this is the case even for people who created the changes—but you can find out how many of them are affected by it.

I like to start with the weekly goal of finding a handful of companies that you would be potentially interested in working for. From there, plan out whom you will network with. Many of the experts I spoke with recommend reaching out to hiring managers from that company (whom you can find through LinkedIn searches) or recruiters who are handling the hiring. You might be asking yourself, "Why not talk to people who hold the job I want to learn more about it?" You will do that eventually, but for now, you want to talk to people who have big-picture perspectives.

Hiring managers often have the insider scoop on whether a company will be hiring in the future, which is one reason why you shouldn't target only companies that are actively hiring. Meghan Conaty told me that she sometimes interviews folks before they've seen a job description. She will align them with a job after she meets them. Recruiters are also always looking to form long-term relationships; they might not have something for you right now, but five years down the line, don't be surprised if you hear from them again.

Next, reach out to current or past employees of those companies

Naturally you will want to ask about your ideal preference list from the people who hold the job you want to hold. During this time, you might be tempted to talk to as many people as possible. But I was advised repeatedly by the folks who hire that exercising restraint at this stage is best. If you don't yet understand the structure of the organization, you might be reaching out to the

wrong people. Ethan Mao recommends asking the hiring manager or recruiter, "Would you have the ability to set me up with
someone already in this position, so I don't potentially message
the wrong person?" or "Who is the best person to speak with internally to explore more opportunities?"

As you start reaching out to people, you want to form a network that includes a broad range of companies (I would start with
three), with three to four contacts within each company. Keep
track of how many of those contacts know one another. Network
density—the degree to which each contact in your network knows
another contact in it—can affect how much information overlap
you end up with, a topic I discussed in the Crisis of Identity chapter. Some information overlap is good; if you talk to three people
who all worked for the same boss, you can gain insight into how
similar their experiences were. But too much overlap can make it
difficult for you to generalize about people's experiences. If you
spoke to three people who not only work for the same company,
but also recruited one another, they might have too much information overlap. Perhaps all those people have three of your five
must-haves, but their experiences don't generalize to anyone who
is not part of that small clique. The only way to find out is to reach
out to more people.

Keep track of shared and unshared experiences

Once you start seeing themes around whether your must-have
preferences exist in a job, and how stable that preference is, you
should keep track of how much consensus there is in people's an-

swers. This way, you have data not only on whether a company provides your must-haves and how stable they are, but also on whether multiple people within that company have a similar must-have experience. This seems obvious, but don't rely on your memory of these chats. Write down what you've learned as soon as you learn it.

Stage three: Go on a fact-finding mission to test whether a career is a good fit for you

The goal of stage two is to learn about the organizations you're interested in working for. In stage three, you will learn how to ask the right questions during the application and interview process to make sure that a position is a good fit for you. For the Drifted Apart, the key theme of this process is making sure that the job you wind up taking aligns with the one you were promised. By this point, you know what you want, but you need to carefully assess whether a job you're applying and interviewing for can give it to you.

While doing research for this book I discovered an interesting pattern: miscommunications between hiring professionals and job seekers are frequent, and often start off small, yet over time lead to divergent expectations of what a job ought to be. Small missteps—like failing to ask how involved your future manager was in the creation of the job ad or why a position is vacant—add up. It's easy to spend weeks in interviews with people who will never actually oversee you at work.

There are multiple stages in a relationship with your job in which these miscommunications can arise, and stage three is organized around detecting them in each stage. Most of us understand the life course of miscommunications from our experience in romantic relationships. Early on during the impression management phase, miscommunications arise when people aren't fully honest about small preferences, like how much they really enjoy their partner's cooking. Later, once the relationship matures and they no longer pretend to like overcooked steak, they miscommunicate over bigger issues, like wanting children and how much money they should be saving each month. The same pattern happens with your relationship with your job: miscommunications start very early, at the creation of the job advertisement, and continue to unfold during the interview stage. But the good news is, there are clear questions you can ask to make sure you don't fall into a miscommunication trap.

THE JOB ADVERTISEMENT

Who Wrote It?

Most of us think that job advertisements are written, or at least have been seen by, the people who will oversee us at work. I was surprised to learn that this is often not the case. In fact, many job descriptions are written by people who work in human resources and oversee the hiring and onboarding process. Many experts I spoke with aren't convinced these descriptions are bespoke enough to accurately reflect what a job entails. According to William Tincup, job descriptions are often created by "going to Career Builder or Indeed, cutting, copying, and massaging a couple of points, and that's it."

The process of job advertisement creation is also iterative, and it's common for an organization to take an advertisement down, revise it, and put it back up. In the optimal case, this happens when candidates reveal new and interesting skills that they have during the interview process, hiring managers reevaluate the skill sets they think they care about, and new ads are created that ostensibly align more closely with what a company wants in a candidate.

The solution to detecting this issue is simple. Ask who wrote it, whether your future boss was consulted when it was created, and how many times it's been taken down and reposted. Interviewers rarely offer up this information unsolicited, but most agree that it's fair game to ask.

The Interview

I return to the interview again in stage four—how to land the job—but as a quick refresher, here are five critical questions I introduced you to in the Crisis of Identity chapter, which you should also ask here. The goal of these questions is to make sure that your expectations align with what is delivered. As a reminder, those questions are:

What is the goal of the interview?

How did the job come to be?

How much have you interfaced with the hiring manager?

Can you please provide me with a sense of what the day-to-day of the job will look like?

Can I interview at the office (if there is one)?

Stage four: Landing the job you will love

In stage three, I focused on the questions you should ask to increase the likelihood that your expectations align with what will be delivered. In stage four, I switch from the perspective of the job seeker to the job hirer. Like you, they have a list of must-haves. How can you make sure that what you have to offer aligns with what they're looking for?

FRAME YOUR SKILLS IN A WAY THAT MAXIMIZES FIT

The Drifted Apart are experienced career goers, and with that experience comes a diverse skill set. They also know what it looks like when their skills are maximized—used in a way that both facilitates their performance and the performance of those who work with them. This is all good news. It's always easier to tailor a résumé and cover letter for a job when you know what you're good at and you know what you want.

Most hirers I spoke with highlighted how important it is to showcase how you helped achieve a big goal, either for your team or the company directly. I recommend you highlight these high-level achievements, but do so wisely. Many recruiters told me that overselling your contributions is one of the biggest missteps experienced career goers make.

What does an oversell look like? Here are a few examples that the hirers I spoke with told me are relatively common.

One, we present real outcomes, but we oversell how much we contributed to those outcomes. For example, imagine writing on your résumé, "My team contributed to a 56.8 percent increase in customer acquisition for the business." If you were on the team that contributed to the increase, but only for two weeks, this is an oversell. As a consequence, the hiring manager might assume more knowledge of customer acquisition than you have.

Two, the experience we present is real, but much more limited in scope than the résumé suggests. This happens when we use jargon terms like "expert" that imply a level of expertise we don't have. There's no explicit dishonesty here, but there is an implied level of deep knowledge that might not exist. One way to know if you would truly be considered an "expert" given your experience is to ask. In stage two, ask your networking connections, "I have experience doing X. Am I justified in calling myself an expert on my résumé if I were to apply for a job at your company?" There are norms around who gets to call themselves an expert, and the only way to learn them is to ask around.

To prevent overselling, Ethan Mao suggests highlighting boundary conditions of your expertise in interviews. He looks for statements like "Here's what I've done. But to be honest with you . . . ," followed by what you need to work on, or what you want training on. It's okay to mention areas for improvement, and a lot of interviewers like Ethan look for it. Many see it as a red flag if you don't.

If you aren't sure how to frame your skills in a way that will get the attention of hirers, check out the Crisis of Identity chapter, where I do a deep dive on how to frame your skills, with an emphasis on using the right insider language and key terms.

MAKE SURE YOUR SKILLS ARE BEING FULLY EVALUATED DURING THE INTERVIEW

It's tough to find an interviewer who observes your job skills during the interview process. For the Drifted Apart, who at this stage are confident in what skills they want to bring with them to their next job, making sure these skills are being fully evaluated is key to landing a job that fits.

Most interviewers ask you about your skills, but few take an in vivo approach to seeing them in action. If a company decides to hire you because they need you to debug one hundred lines of code in one hundred seconds, and they have you do just that in the interview, rest assured your job will look a lot like what you expect it to. The closer the interview comes to assessing your relevant skills, the less likely you'll be assigned jobs you have no business doing.

In some cases, you're so eager to get out of your current job, vague platitudes like "You would be a great culture fit here!" feel like music to your ears. Fight the urge to say yes if you get an offer after an interview process that feels superficial. Instead, push for your skills to be formally evaluated. Remember, you want to land a job that you won't drift apart from.

How can you do this? Meghan Conaty suggests two steps. First, ask the question "Where do you see me fitting in the organization?" The person interviewing you should know about the organization's structure. You're much less likely to drift apart again if you have a clearly defined role and the company knows what skills are required in that role. If they can't describe what your role will be within the broader structure of the organization, or how your role interfaces with other roles, be wary.

Second, ask the question "How will my technical skills be evaluated during the interview process?" Sometimes you take a job that doesn't fit because the person who interviewed you fell in love with your personality. If you're a charismatic person, congratulations, job interviews probably feel easier for you than for the rest of us. But the failure to sample the skills you need for the job won't benefit you in the long run. Meghan has people go through a case study: "It's an hour-and-a-half interview, and they discuss how they would approach the problem. They're not going to solve the thing, but we want to see how they approach it. Usually, the interviewer will try to push feedback toward them at one point to see how they receive it." Where Meghan works, handling feedback well is a skill people need to have, so they measure it in the interview.

For some jobs, the only way to truly evaluate a candidate's skills is to put them through a scenario that perfectly matches what they will do on the job. One hiring expert I spoke with, Dan

Heasman, has spent years crafting the perfect "skills sampling" interview. He likes to fully immerse the candidate and the hiring committee in an experience that mirrors the job. Like asking to interview in the office, the goal here is to give you a sense of what your day-to-day will look like. You have your must-have list and they have theirs; the "experiential interview" can help make sure the two are aligned.

LEARN HOW TO TELL A GOOD (BUT TRUE) PERSONAL STORY

Most of us spend a lot of time preparing for how we're going to impress people during interviews. A lot of that effort goes into storytelling, at least in the United States. Most jobs don't require you to have Malcolm Gladwell–level storytelling skills, but that doesn't stop interviewers from putting a lot of stock into a good lesson-learned tale. Much of this comes from the popular STAR method, in which people describe a situation they were in, the task they were doing, the actions they took to address the situation, and the result. In one of my surveys of hirers, 42 percent said they had used the STAR method during interviews.

Many recruiters I spoke with have told candidates that if they don't improve their storytelling skills, they won't land a job (and many times, they've been right). The pressure is so intense that when we don't have good material, we start to make it up.

"A lot of people will embellish," Meghan told me. Sometimes, the lies are arbitrary. She remembers one candidate who made up a story that involved when she walked in college graduation, but upon being pushed for details it became clear she never walked. Another one pretended to like opera for her story. She hated opera. And once the lies were detected, these candidates were removed from further consideration.

As a Drifted Apart career goer, you have a lot of experience to draw from. The key is framing that experience in a lesson-learned way that doesn't undercut your past employer. In stage one, I had you walk through what aspects of the job changed in a way that led to your disengagement at work. I also helped you reflect on what changed about you. Draw from these themes to craft a story about what you learned about yourself. And if you're unsure of whether your story hits the mark, ask a hirer in your network during stage two. Many are willing to give feedback—they want you to succeed as much as you do.

▪ ▪

TAKE-HOMES FOR EACH STAGE

STAGE ONE:

- Document the changes you've experienced in your day-to-day using the Changes to My Job checklist.

- Remember that organizational-level changes impact these changes, but most of us don't agree on how (including the people who helped orchestrate them).

- Focus on how you, too, have changed at work by going through my preferences exercise: "I used to prefer X, and now I prefer Y."

STAGE TWO:

- Focus on getting answers to three questions: One, do I have a good sense of how quickly my industry is changing, not just my job? Two, if yes, are the changes to my industry so drastic that I might want to consider a career change? And three, if I do want to stay in this career, how likely is it that I will find all my must-haves in one place?

- Network with multiple people who work within the organization you're considering so you can find out how likely it is that a change within the organization can impact the possibility that your must-have will still be around in the future.

STAGE THREE:

- Ask questions around the job advertisement, including who wrote it and how many times it has been taken down and put back up, to help detect miscommunications within the organization that is hiring you.

- Ask the five critical questions I introduced in the Crisis of Identity chapter.

STAGE FOUR:

- Frame your skills without overselling them, focusing on how you've contributed to team- or company-level outcomes, if relevant.

- Make sure your skills are fully evaluated during the interview (and ask how they will be in the early interview stages).

- Learn to tell a good but true personal story.

THE STRETCHED TOO THIN

I'm everywhere all at once,
and the juggle isn't sustainable

Jake, a data analyst at a bank, sat in the corner of his own party, nervously drinking a glass of scotch. The company president had blasted out an email earlier that day congratulating him on his big promotion, but Jake was in no mood to celebrate.

"I'm supposed to be excited that they fired my boss and I have to take over her job?" he said to no one in particular. "No, thank you."

In this age of constant layoffs and inflation, a lot of people think that yes, Jake should be grateful. Sure, he was handed a ton of new responsibilities, including overseeing a team of twelve. But he was also given the fancy title of "Director," a raise, and an assistant to help him with the transition. For the Runner-Up and the Underappreciated Star—the topics of the next two chapters of this book—Jake's job sounds like a dream.

But there was more going on with Jake than simply not being excited. He seemed downright afraid of the promotion.

I spent some time trying to figure out why.

"Every day from eight to ten a.m. I sit alone at my computer and do 'deep work,'" Jake told me. A master of self-restraint, Jake learned to accomplish more during this two-hour window than most of us get done in a day. No work emails, calls, or casual conversations allowed. And critically, no task switching.

The rest of each day—from ten a.m. until around four p.m.—he did the other stuff that most of us count as work. Meetings, emails, catching up on paperwork. He was interrupted constantly, but that was okay. Because he was so good at getting the important stuff done early, he almost never worked after hours.

Jake had known for years that it's not just *what* you do at work that can make you feel like you're stretched too thin, it's *how* you do it. "You can have two people who have the exact same five tasks they have to juggle, and one succeeds, and one fails. And the reason why I succeed is because I know my shortcomings, and I know how to structure my time. No one is 'smart' all day," he tells me. "I make sure to do the stuff that requires real thinking during that one small block of time in the morning."

I understand Jake's concern. As a writer, I also block off my "smart time," and the thought of losing that two-hour window feels like an existential threat. Jake's identity with his career is anchored to the "deep work" he does, not the emails, paper pushing, or meetings.

For those who've survived the low point of a relationship, when you're overworked with caregiving or working until midnight, with no time or energy left to spend on intimacy, you know how important that two-hour block can be. It's a natural progression, going from Stretched Too Thin to Drifted Apart, and eventually to having a Crisis of Identity.

And for Jake, that's what happened.

About a month after his promotion, I caught up with him to see how the transition was going. "At first I tried to keep my morning routine," he told me. He didn't get a lot of outside interruptions, which was a nice surprise. "But then I started to break my own rules. One time, I couldn't stop thinking about this big meeting I had at eleven a.m., so I would stop my work and go through my notes again to make sure I felt prepared." Then came communicating with the outside world. "Once my team saw that I was hopping on Slack during those two hours, they started bugging me nonstop." The amount of deep work time shrank from two hours to one. And by the end of two weeks, it was gone completely.

Jake tried to make up the time in the evenings, but it turned him into an insomniac, and before long he was on leave. For now, his plan is to look for an individual contributor role, which means less money and no assistant, but the ability to protect his two-hour mornings. "There's really no set of perks that can make up for that lost time," he said. "If someone really wants you to take on a role that involves juggling a million things, be honest with yourself about what trade-offs you're willing to make. If they come to you and say, 'We will give you more money or a better title,' but it will mean having no control over your time, think hard about that."

▪ ▪ ▪

What is a Stretched Too Thin career goer?

One of the main reasons why people leave their job and seek out another is because they are Stretched Too Thin. They don't have the resources to cope with the demands of the day, either because they are handed more roles than they can handle and toggling between them isn't feasible, or because they task switch so often that they rarely finish what they start—or both. For some, being stretched too thin is inherent to the job. Medical practitioners, especially those who work in emergency departments, often feel this way. For others, being stretched too thin isn't a product of what they do at work, but how they do it. As Jake illustrated, *how* we spend our time working is just as important as *what* we spend our time working on. Interruptions at work, like closing a browser you're working in to open a new one, or stopping midsentence in a document to have a chat with a colleague, can be just as disruptive to your work as hopping from meeting to meeting without a break.

These disruptions cost you more than your productivity. They can lead you to start to psychologically distance yourself from your job, and to feel bitter and trapped. Ironically, the things we love most about our jobs are often the first on the chopping block when we feel stretched too thin. This happened to Jake, and it's happened to me many times in my career, when my time spent doing research gets eaten up by paper pushing and committee meetings. When I don't get to work on the stuff I care about, my mood sours and my identity as a professor starts to wane. I've learned to put steps in place to protect the parts of my job I most strongly identify with so I don't turn into a Crisis of Identity career goer. In relationship therapy, this lesson is one of the first you'll learn: Protect the time in the relationship that is key to keeping intimacy alive. It's often the first to go when you feel stressed, but it's the most important.

If you feel burned out and overwhelmed at work and you need some tips on how to organize your workload, then this chapter is for you. Not every chapter in this book is meant for everyone, but this one is, even if you aren't thinking about leaving your career. Much of the advice I give will not only help you figure out how to find a future job in which being Stretched Too Thin is less likely, but it can also help you become more productive and less stressed at your current job, should you choose to stay. You might find that as you develop your productivity skills and stop saying yes to new tasks, your job becomes enjoyable again and you aren't rushing to leave it. But critically, learning these productivity skills can help you protect the parts of your career that keep you strongly identified with it, even if you do want to switch organizations for a change but stick with your industry.

Stage one: Why am I unhappy here?

In stage one—figuring out why you're unhappy at work—I focus on two big questions: One, am I taking on too many roles or responsibilities at work? And two, am I interrupted so much during the workday that I'm having a hard time getting anything done? This stage is oriented around the practicalities of the job, but if, like Jake, you feel yourself de-identifying with your career, I strongly urge you to keep track of whether the work that's not getting done is identity-related. Perhaps that's an hour a day of strategic planning, or in my case, at least a few hours a week of research. Not all work is created equal, and knowing whether the work that's taking a hit is the meaning-making kind is an important part of discovering why you're unhappy. For people whose jobs inherently involve juggling multiple tasks, this question is especially weighty. You might have little control over the degree to which you have to task switch, but you need to find out whether the meaning-making work is being pushed to the side.

As you answer these questions, you will also want to uncover how much control you have over what you work on and how you work. For example, when it comes to the roles or responsibilities you have, are you volunteering to take on extra jobs, or are these things assigned to you? And when it comes to interruptions, how often are other people interrupting you (a boss tells you to stop what you're doing to help him), and how often are you interrupting yourself (you chose to check your email in the middle of working on something)?

Let's consider each question in turn.

Am I taking on too many roles or responsibilities at work?

According to the World Economic Forum, 80 percent of us hold multiple roles at work. As I illustrated in the Crisis of Identity chapter, the biggest category of "Nobody told me that" answers were extra responsibilities.

But some roles are more important than others, and sometimes we take on extra roles that we don't have the bandwidth to do because we think they will give us a leg up at work.

To illustrate, I asked 201 people to describe the roles they have at work, which include things they do and don't get paid to do. The average number of roles people held was a little over five, with 30 percent of the sample having more than six roles, and 15 percent having ten. I then asked people whether they were "assigned this position at work" or whether they "volunteered for it," meaning they did the work for free. Last, I asked them why they took on each role, with a checklist of options. You can do the same exercise for yourself. Write out your roles and whether they're part of your paid job, and, on the list below, check why you take on each.

Here's that list:

- ☐ It's the job I was hired to do.
- ☐ To help out a colleague who is falling behind.
- ☐ Because others aren't doing their jobs and I'm picking up the slack.
- ☐ There is no one else to do it.
- ☐ There are other people who can do it, but I'm the best person for it.
- ☐ I was elected to do it in a vote at work.

☐ It helps my reputation.

☐ It gives me a chance to connect with people at work I would otherwise not connect with.

☐ It's important for my career development.

☐ It gives me opportunities I would otherwise not have.

☐ It impresses the person who asked me to do it.

☐ It impresses people in power.

☐ I had no choice. I was told I had to.

☐ I felt guilty saying no.

☐ I was worried that if I said no, I might get laid off or fired.

☐ I was told that this responsibility is temporary.

☐ Everyone at this organization takes on multiple roles and responsibilities.

☐ I'm only asked to do it when the person responsible for it is out for the day/week/month.

☐ I was handed this role/responsibility when the person whose job it was left the organization.

☐ I do it because it gives my work meaning.

In my data, over 25 percent of people took on multiple roles because doing so is the norm at the organization where they work, and 59 percent of people had at least one role they weren't getting paid to do. Most of us are taking on too much because everyone else around us is doing it. If this is you, ask yourself, "Is this inherent to my job, or is this something that is unique to my organization?"

I also found that across all roles people took on, 24 percent were volunteer jobs. The amount of time people spent doing volunteer work isn't trivial; on average, they spent about twenty-one hours a week per role they were assigned (and paid) to do, and eleven hours on each volunteer role. It also seems to be the case that taking paid roles leads to volunteer ones: the likelihood of doing at least one volunteer role went up 63 percent for every paid role a person took on!

The question is, why are people doing so much work for free?

In my study, people indicated that they frequently took on a volunteer role because they think it will increase their visibility at work; around 32 percent of people think these volunteer roles helped their reputation at work. We often volunteer for jobs that we think will help us gain status.

If you fall into this category, think carefully about your assumptions of what that role will buy you. Not all roles at work will gain you the visibility you need. In fact, many do just the opposite; they suck you away from the work that really matters. If people are asking you to take on these so-called visibility roles, ask yourself why. Newcomers or people who don't know the hidden curriculum are often cajoled into taking "highly visible" but not "high-status" jobs. In some professions, such as human resources, this practice is the norm. The promise of visibility and influence—of the chance to network with people in multiple parts of the organization—is a siren song that lures people in. Yet taking on jobs that are associated with visibility—everyone knows you're doing it—but which don't bring you respect and influence is one of the biggest predictors of turnover at work. Once people realize that this strategy isn't helping them climb up, they leave.

If you checked several of the visibility items in my measure, you might already fall into the category of taking on jobs primarily because they make you visible at work. In stages two and three, I will teach you how to test your assumptions that a job will give you the kind of visibility you need to get ahead. Your networking connections can tell you if a role or responsibility will give you the right type of visibility (it will showcase your skills to the people in power), or the wrong type (it gives you the reputation of saying yes to everything, even the pointless jobs).

Here's an example from my own life. I was recently asked to be on the university promotion committee, which is a ton of work. When I asked around about whether it was worth it, I got a lot of swift yeses. One person gave me a clear explanation as to why: "Being on the promotion committee exposes the deans to your reasoning skills, which they will want to see in action before promoting you to the role of chair." Chair is a position of power, and this role gives decision-makers important data for making sure the person they're assigning to that role is a good fit. If the answer had been "It feels like a big deal, but it's a ton of work and no one in power keeps track of who does it," I would have turned it down.

But there are other reasons why people take on unpaid work.

I'm the only logical choice

Two items measure the "logical choice" reasons for taking on a role: "there is no one else to do it" (21 percent) and "there are other people to do it, but I'm the best person for the job" (15 percent).

If you checked off one of the "logical choice" items, you will want to ask yourself two questions: One, is it really the case that

I'm the only person for this job? And two, if yes, what are the structural features of the workplace that enable this form of being spread too thin? Is it inherent to the career, or just this particular job?

I run a leadership training workshop, and one of the exercises I have people go through is "tricky situations at work." One of the most common situations that leaders complain about is people overworking themselves by volunteering for work they really have no business doing, but that they think no one else can do. (Often it's the case that others want to do the work, but the overeager employee convinces them not to.) Leaders are constantly managing this form of self-induced burnout. People who do this are often trying to impress the boss, but in some cases, they are the boss.

Many of the people in my study who responded to being the only person for the job also thought the job gave them visibility. These two sources of being stretched too thin overlap. If you're unsure whether you're the best person for the (volunteer) work, set up a feedback meeting with your team or your boss. You can start with a simple question: "Lately I've been volunteering to do [insert your job here]. Do you think this work should be allocated to someone else, or do you think I'm the best person for it, and why?"

No, really, I am the only logical choice

Naturally, there are times when indeed there really is no one else to do a job. Often, these "optionless" roles take the place of our meaning-making ones. Before we know it, they've eaten up the time we spend on the stuff we care about. I've noticed that when I don't have time to work on my research, it's almost always because I'm chairing a job search or heading some other decision-making committee that I was asked to take on by a leader. And almost always I do these things because someone has come along and told me that I'm the only logical choice.

I might research these things, but I'm just as susceptible to making these mistakes as you are.

There are some organizations in which you are more likely to run into this problem, regardless of your industry, like those with a flat hierarchy that has an "all hands on deck" mentality. It doesn't matter how high up you are, you're expected to absorb the workload of others when the company is short-staffed. Be wary of working for an organization with a business model like this. Hierarchies serve an important function; they create clearly defined roles and, within the roles, clearly defined tasks.

I'm correcting for free riders

Two items measure "free-rider correction" reasons for taking on a role: "to help a colleague who is falling behind" (16 percent) and because "others aren't doing their jobs and I'm picking up the slack" (9 percent). Presumably people are volunteering for jobs that others are getting paid to do.

I was surprised to learn that among the people who checked these boxes, most work in teams where there's a system in place to keep track of the work of each team member. Usually, free riding is more common on teams where there's no such system. In a strange twist, the people in my study are correcting for free riders on these teams because they think that, despite not getting compensated for the work, they will at least get social recognition for it. Imagine that Mark agreed to finish his report by Tuesday, he didn't do it, and you did it for him (even though he's the one who got paid for it). Presumably you can then brag to the team at the next meeting, "Guess who finished that report for Mark? I did." I don't recommend this strategy. People rarely get formally recognized for picking up the slack of free riders, at least not by the people in power.

I'm interrupted so much, I'm having a hard time getting anything done

Now let's turn to the next source of being stretched too thin: being interrupted so much that you can't get anything done. Here are some depressing data for you.

The average worker experiences eighty-six workplace interruptions a day. In fact, we spend about two hours a day at work just on being interrupted—a problem that costs the U.S. economy at least $588 billion annually. We are in the most distracted moment in human history.

The good news is, we have more control over how and when we're interrupted than we think. Some interruptions are external; a chatty coworker pops over to talk, or a boss asks for your last-minute help on a meeting prep. But others are internal; we choose to minimize one work program to open another; we stop writing midsentence to answer a text.

Just how common are these different types of interruptions? I asked the 201 people in my study, "In thinking about your day, did you have anything on your to-do list that you didn't complete?" Around 38 percent of people said yes. Next, I asked them to list three things on their to-do list that they didn't complete at the end of the workday. For each, they were given a checklist of reasons why.

Here's that list:

These six reasons are *internal* disruptions:

☐ I minimized the program or tab I was working in and opened up another program or tab to work on something else.

☐ I checked my work email or work Slack (or other form of work communication).

☐ I checked my social media, including Facebook, Twitter, LinkedIn, Instagram, or other social media.

☐ I decided to move to a new physical space.

☐ I stopped working to get food or a drink.

☐ I got up to go do something else not work-related (e.g., go for a walk).

These eight reasons are *external* disruptions:

- ☐ Someone at work stopped by and interrupted me in person to ask a work-related question.
- ☐ Someone asked if I wanted to take a break with them (e.g., go get coffee).
- ☐ Someone at work called or texted.
- ☐ Someone told me to stop what I was doing mid-task and switch to something more urgent.
- ☐ I was forced to leave the physical space I was in (e.g., other people came in to occupy the room, and it got too loud).
- ☐ I ran out of time and had to go do something else (e.g., go to a meeting, go home).
- ☐ A family member or someone in my personal life interrupted me.
- ☐ I was in transit when working and had to stop for travel reasons (e.g., I had to put away a laptop because a plane was taking off or I had to get off a train).

The next time you're at work, document three tasks you didn't get done and why. How many of these sources of interruption are internal—things you do to yourself—versus external—things done to you by other people?

In my data, among the top six most frequent interruptions, four were internal and two were external. The most common interruption was checking work email or Slack (3 times per task), followed by minimizing a program to work on something else (2.5 times per task).

By and large, when we're interrupted at work, we do it to ourselves. If this is you, you might be feeling pressure to engage in self-interruptions—you know that an important email from your boss is coming in and you have no choice but to respond to it. Evaluating how much pressure you're under to self-interrupt is an important step. And if you're not under external pressure, consider how often your self-interruptions are triggered by a stressor at work. For example, Jake's anxiety about his performance on an upcoming presentation led him to violate his own work rules. My weakness is being late on something. One small stress cue— like glancing at my calendar and realizing something was due two weeks ago—is enough for me to switch gears completely to get the thing off my desk. My strategy works to regulate my stress in the moment, but ironically it can lead to more stress down the road.

As you go through this process, keep in mind that we all have moments of weakness when we prioritize something we shouldn't. We're like the workaholic who secretly answers her boss's call during a date-night dinner; in the moment it reduces our anxiety about disappointing our boss, but the damage it does to the relationship might not be worth it.

Are interruptions affecting my ability to pick up where I left off?

After you understand the source of your interruptions, the next step is to understand the full scope of how they're affecting your work. Interruptions do more than just influence our ability to get something done in the moment. They also influence our ability to pick up where we left off.

To understand why, I spoke to neuroscientist Dr. Lila Davachi about how interruptions affect our ability to form new memories. At work, we form episodic memories of small things, like what paragraphs you wrote in a document (if you're a writer), or what notes you took about a client (if you're a therapist). But our ability to form memories of these tasks is often disrupted. In fact, about 41 percent of the tasks we interrupted doing aren't resumed immediately. When this happens, your brain has a hard time creating an "episode" of the work you've done.

What are the implications of this process for the chronically interrupted?

"*Any* kind of distraction—checking email, people walking in to ask questions—disrupts your internal pattern of stability, making it harder to create rich, temporarily integrated memories," Dr. Davachi told me.

Imagine that you're working on an important writing assignment at work, and you've spent the last three hours going in and out of the document, checking your email or editing another document in another window on your computer. These internal interruptions not only impact your ability to complete the assignment, but also to encode what you wrote (and why). The next time you open the document, you will probably find yourself scratching your head and thinking, "Why did I write that again?"

The work of Dr. Davachi shows us that any form of interruption can disrupt our ability to form memories at a deep, neural level. And although we don't think about being stretched too thin as a memory problem per se, it is.

Jake understood this. His two-hour morning block was critical to his productivity for multiple reasons. Not only did it allow him to do deep work in the moment, but it was during this time that he created rich, integrated memories of the work he was doing. The next day when he started again, he could easily recall those memories and get back into it.

To understand how disruptive interruptions are to your progress, document how hard it is to jump back in

What I've learned from Dr. Davachi is not only how important it is to document the source of our interruptions in the moment, but also how difficult it is to jump back into a task later on. Start by documenting three things: when you started a task, the interruptions you experienced during it, and how difficult it was to return to the task. I documented up my own experience writing this book (during a small window of time by myself, in a hotel room).

After documenting my interruptions for several days, I noticed a pattern. I experienced the greatest difficulty jumping back into my writing when two things happened: one, I experienced a handful of interruptions (most of which were internal); and two, I worked on writing only once a day. The combination of small interruptions plus a long lag time between work sessions made progress difficult.

Once I understood this pattern, I was better at constructing my work schedule. If I experience a handful of interruptions during my morning work time, I make sure to spend at least thirty minutes writing at the end of the day to jog my memory.

Started task	Interruptions	Returned to task
Time: 8–10 a.m. **Context:** Alone in hotel room	**Internal (3):** Made phone call at 8:45 Checked email at 9:15 Made coffee at 9:45 **External (0):** none	**Time:** 3 p.m. (same day) **Difficulty:** Minimal; started where I left off
Time: 8–10 a.m. (next day) **Context:** Alone in hotel room	**Internal (2):** Checked email at 8:30, 10 **External (1):** Cleaning people came, went to the gym at 9:45	**Time:** 8 a.m. (next day) **Difficulty:** Hard. Had to reread research by Dr. Lila Davachi that I spent an hour reading the prior day.

Stage two: What do I want my future career to look like?

By the end of stage one, you will start to have answers to two main questions I proposed at the start of this chapter: why you're taking on roles at work (and how many are done in the service of increasing visibility), and what the source is of your daily interruptions. In addition, I urged you to focus on whether the tasks you're falling behind on are meaning-making ones that foster a sense of identity. You might find that after going through the stage one exercises, you can solve your Stretched Too Thin problems by reorganizing how you work and taking control over your own internal interruptions (and the unnecessary roles you're taking on). If, however, you realize that you don't have control over either the roles you're asked to take on or the nature of your interruptions at work, or both, then it's time to move on to stage two.

The first step of stage two is to work on prioritizing roles so you know what jobs to search for in stage three. Much like the Crisis of Identity career goer, the Stretched Too Thin career goer will need to do some soul searching to figure out which roles are central to their career identity, and which they want to anchor their future job search on.

RANK YOUR ROLES, FROM MOST TO LEAST RELEVANT TO YOUR CAREER

In the Crisis of Identity chapter, I introduced you to the idea of identity centrality and identity satisfaction: centrality captures how central an identity is to you, and satisfaction is how much joy that identity brings you. You can think about your roles at work in a similar way in this chapter: Which ones do you identify the most strongly with, and which bring you the most satisfaction? Like the identity questions, these questions get at the heart of where you see yourself going in the future. But they do differ in one critical way: they assume that you have a central career identity that you want to keep; it's the roles that fall under the umbrella of that identity that need some fine-tuning.

I had people in the same study go through this exercise, and 89 percent of people could rank their most and least important role (the remainder said they were equally important). Despite having a lot of roles, people can pick the ones they care about the most.

When I looked at the roles people held, I found they mostly mapped onto one of the following three categories: day-to-day roles, up-and-out roles, and passion roles.

Imagine, for example, that you have a strong identity as a school-teacher, but you feel overwhelmed by the three roles you're juggling—classroom teaching, curriculum building, and serving as the local representative for the teachers union.

Day-to-day roles get at the meat of your day-to-day work. These roles take up the most time and have the greatest impact on your daily stress. The teacher who prioritizes in-classroom teaching falls into this category. This person cares about things that influence where they spend most of their time: student-to-teacher ratio, classroom resources like in-room tech, and availability of in-class aides. These are the roles we are typically hired to do and that we see as central to our job.

Up-and-out roles help you move beyond your current position. People who hold these roles score high on the visibility subscale I introduced above. The teacher who cares about curriculum building might want to hold a position of leadership in education one day, like becoming a principal or superintendent. Working with people in multiple schools, including administrators, gives them exposure to the people who will help them achieve this goal.

Passion roles are often tangential to your main role at work. The teacher who prioritizes work as the union rep falls into this category. These roles give people meaning at work. Some people see them as "important to career development," but this is an assumption you will want to test during networking. Just because you think it ought to help your career progress doesn't mean it will. If most of the roles that make it to the top of your list are passion roles, you should think about whether you fall into the category of the Crisis of Identity career goer. If what you're spending your time on doesn't align with what will get you paid or advance your career, you might want to consider a career change.

CAN YOU ORGANIZE YOUR WORK IN TERMS OF WORKING SPHERES?

All jobs contain multiple roles and responsibilities; it's nearly impossible to escape this modern workplace reality. But some roles have more overlap than others in terms of the contexts in which they are done and the tacit knowledge needed to complete them. Managing multiple roles is easier when we can stay within what scientists call working spheres—broad categories of work that encompass multiple roles and are organized around high-level units of work. Big projects, like a pitch for a client, or in my case designing a research study or writing a book proposal, would be considered working spheres. High-level units of work are things like doing research for the chapter on the Spread Too Thin career goer.

Gloria Mark and her colleagues studied the behaviors of workers at an outsourcing company who juggled multiple roles. After observing the day-to-day activities of employees for over seven hundred hours, the authors discovered that the employees who were the most productive didn't refrain entirely from task switching, but when they did it, it was almost aways *within* a working sphere. They didn't task switch across them. For example, if I'm working today on writing my book (one sphere), and I must task switch, I should go from analyzing data for the book to writing text in a chapter. What I shouldn't do is task switch between working spheres, even if the task feels similar—like going from writing text for my book to writing text for a paper. It's a bit counterintuitive.

The authors also discovered that people who were able to juggle a lot had roles that cut across working spheres. For me, the role of writer is relevant to the sphere of book writing and the sphere of conducting research. If I had to start from scratch, using a new set of skills or knowledge every time I started writing in a new sphere, I would be in trouble. I've chosen a career with a lot of role overlap.

To organize your work in terms of working spheres, try this approach. At the start of the day, write out what spheres you will work in. Today I will work on my book (sphere one), undergraduate teaching (sphere two), and the hiring committee (sphere three). Then write out the tasks you need to do within each sphere. Don't be too ambitious—the goal is to finish the work within the sphere for that day, not interrupt yourself when you realize time has run out and you need to start working in a new sphere. For my three spheres, that means editing one chapter, reading three student papers, and rating ten job applicants. Extra tasks that don't fall within a sphere, like meetings and emails, should be done when you've completed the work within a sphere. Think of these things as sphere breaks.

NETWORKING BASED ON YOUR ROLE PRIORITIES

I've given you a lot of lessons on how to be productive while jug-gling multiple roles, but ultimately, if you're not happy with your job and you want to start looking for a new one, this is how you should network to make sure you don't take on a new job that will have the same set of problems as your current one.

In stage two, you will want to network with people who can help you gain clarity on what the day-to-day looks like for people who hold the role you're primarily interested in, along with some additional questions regarding role overlap that I will get to. But first, whom should you network with?

As we discussed in the Crisis of Identity chapter, most of us have connections with people who work in the same industry as we do. This is good news for you; you will want to network with these industry connections. You can identify the organizations you're interested in first, and then identify people who work in your ideal role, like I recommended to the Drifted Apart in stage two of that chapter. You can also network with people who hold your role across different organizations to decrease the amount of information overlap you get. Norms are often at the organization and team level, especially regarding role overlap, so networking broadly across organizations can help you identify which norms are industry-wide and which are company-specific.

Your main goal should be to identify people within your in-dustry who have the role that you're primarily interested in—the one that rose to the top of your ranking list. You will continue to fine-tune your thinking about roles as you move through this process, but at this stage, you should know what role you care about the most.

Why?

The biggest mistake I've seen Stretched Too Thin career goers make is not anchoring their search on one role from the beginning. It's a bit like the career goer in the Crisis of Identity chapter who has very little identity clarity—they know very broadly what they want to do, but they aren't clear on where they are going and why. Without clear priorities and boundaries around those priorities, you're setting yourself up to be stretched too thin at your next job.

QUESTIONS TO ASK DURING THESE CONVERSATIONS

How much overlap is there in the work you do across these roles?

As I mentioned above, if you take on multiple roles, the skills required in each of these roles should overlap. Ask people if they see connections between the work required for multiple roles. For example, "I see that you hold two main roles—running the internship program and overseeing a team, and you mentioned giving weekly feedback to both as part of your job. Can you use the same feedback structure for both, or do you have to do one thing for the interns and something completely different for your team?" If I were interviewing myself, I would ask, "I see you write a lot. Are the skills you need to write a trade book different from those you need to write academic papers?"

As you go through this process, you will likely uncover some hidden roles that are part of the job, but that you haven't heard of before. It's critical to identify these "not-advertised" roles early so you can ask specific questions about them in stage three.

How much say do you have over your working spheres?

I recommend that you plan out your day in terms of working spheres, but not all jobs afford people that much flexibility. Give people examples of what different working spheres are (remembering that "working sphere" is jargon, so you will need to spell it out), and then ask, "Is it realistic to be able to plan out my day this way?" In fast-paced workplaces where your time is not your own, the answer will likely be no. And even if it's a yes, remember that there will always be times when you need to prioritize one sphere over another. When I have a book deadline looming, that's the only sphere I'm in, often for weeks at a time. Things like constant external interruptions that you can't control will make it tough to stay within a sphere. During chats, pay careful attention to the working spheres you care about the most—the ones that influence your identity and sense of purpose.

Have I categorized roles correctly into the three types?

Last, test whether your understanding of the meaning of roles—whether they are day-to-day, up-and-out, or passion roles—maps onto the experiences of people who hold these roles. I've worked with many career goers who thought passion roles would be more respected by people in their industry than they are. One person came to me with a résumé full of outreach experience working with underprivileged children in education. She had spent months helping youth learn about careers in STEM. The problem was, she wanted a job teaching at a liberal arts school. She had some teaching experience, but not enough to make her competitive for the job, so she wasn't getting any interest. I explained to her that her passion role would not make her stand out in the job market; it made her look like a Crisis of Identity career goer. Eventually she went to work for a nonprofit, which was a much better fit.

Collect the data broadly by asking multiple people to categorize the roles they have into three camps. You want consistency across organizations in how they are labeled; like all other things, there are norms about how important certain roles are for career development that are company specific.

▪ ▪ ▪

Stage three: Go on a fact-finding mission to test whether a career is a good fit for you

By the time you've reached the end of stage two, you will know how the primary role you want to hold looks "in the wild"— including what other roles typically go along with it, and how much overlap there is in the work required to execute all the roles that typically go together. In stage three, the goal is to dig a little deeper to find out what features of the workplace will make or break your success at pulling off multiple roles. Features of the environment, like whether there's an open floor plan and whether people work on the same or different floors, influence your ability to stay within working spheres. Cultural norms, like whether it's okay to create "white space" in your day, influence your ability to do deep work.

For the Stretched Too Thin career goer, stage three is about becoming an anthropologist—learning how to read workplace environments for clues about how people balance their roles and how they manage interruptions. And the best place to start is the physical office.

HOW DOES THE OFFICE LAYOUT INFLUENCE WHEN YOU'RE INTERRUPTED, AND HOW YOU GET BACK TO WORK?

We can learn a lot about workplace culture by observing people in their natural habitats, even if just for a short window of time. Things like whether people eat lunch at their desk or take a break, and how far the managers sit from everyone else, offer insight into norms and routines.

But no career goer benefits from seeing an office environment as much as the Stretched Too Thin. The physical layout offers clues to questions like "How likely is it that I will be interrupted at work?" and "How hard is it for me to stay within a working sphere?" These are important questions to ask during an interview. But answers alone won't get the data you need to make an informed decision. You need to see the environment for yourself.

To illustrate, let's return to the Gloria Mark study I discussed above. I mentioned that the most efficient employees organized their work in terms of working spheres—high-level units of work that include multiple tasks that often cut across roles.

Most people, it turns out, struggled to stay within their working spheres. In fact, 57 percent of people had a working sphere interrupted at least once, when they were pulled out to work on something unrelated. Working spheres that were central to their job were interrupted 83 percent of the time! On average, people spent eleven minutes and four seconds working in a sphere before they were interrupted.

People's physical proximity to other team members offers a clue as to why. The researchers compared people who are colocated (they work in a cubicle with at least one team member in an adjacent cubicle) to those who are evenly distributed (they are physically separated from their teammates, because they work across the room from them, have an enclosed office, or they are in another building). They found that people who work next to each other spend more time in a working sphere than distributed people do, but they are also more likely to be interrupted. What can explain this seemingly contradictory pattern of findings?

Not all interruptions are created equal, and even though people who were close interrupted one another more (it's easy to interrupt people next to you), they were more strategic when they did it. People in cubicles would listen to what their neighbors were doing and only interrupt them during opportune times, like during a lull in their work. The people who worked farther away from one another interrupted when it was convenient for them.

When you interview, ask to see the physical layout of the office and, more important, where you will work relative to others on your team. If your work is hybrid, ask when others are in and where they work. And if you work in a hoteling environment—where the office changes every day—find out how much control you have over who you work close to and whether you can always get the same working space. You need to be able to predict your physical environment on your "in" days so you can plan an interruption schedule with your coworkers. Interruptions are inevitable, but having control over yours is important for creating memories of your work so that later you can pick up where you left off.

CAN YOU CREATE ARTIFACTS IN YOUR OFFICE SPACE?

There's a trend called hot desking that has taken over the hybrid work world, where people reserve a workspace or team room every time they come on-site. Hoteling is similar. The days of having a permanent workspace are dwindling.

But permanent workspaces are important; they give you the opportunity to add your own personal touches, like little clues that help prioritize your work and remind you where you left off. Victor M. Gonzalez and Gloria Mark found that information workers (administrators, managers, financial analysts, consultants, and accountants), who on average worked in ten working spheres a day, relied on these clues to get back into a working sphere when interrupted. Some people put physical folders on their desktop, organized by working sphere. Others printed emails that were in a pile, all belonging to one working sphere. Post-it notes were common, too, full of checklists to document their progress, color coded by sphere. One person smartly created an email subfield called "Z immediate attention issues" so it always appeared at the end of his alphabetically organized inbox.

These clues can help you get back on track when your interruptions are device based—when you go from writing an email to having an in-person conversation, or jotting down something by hand followed by typing something on your laptop. When we shift devices, the natural clues we rely on, like a blinking cursor at the end of a sentence, disappear. Having additional clues, like a color-coded list of priorities handwritten on your white board, makes it easier to get back into the work.

Think of these clues like a trail of breadcrumbs that help us find our way back when we're interrupted. And they aren't just important for getting back to work immediately following an interruption, they are also important for metawork—time spent on organizing our working spheres. Most people spent some time at the end of the day organizing their desks, managing their email subfolders, and checking in with team members on what balls had been dropped. Your piles of emails or whiteboard charts help you organize this metawork.

Remote workers might be thinking, "How does this apply to me? I don't have a hot desk or a cool hotel I can work in each day."

It certainly does apply to you. Many remote workers don't have a permanent workspace or office at home—they work in the kitchen or the bedroom, or anywhere that's quiet. We think of our home environments as flexible these days—the kitchen table can be where we chop vegetables, play a game with our kids, or write a report. If you work in multiple places (or your workspace turns into the dinner table at six), you need to make sure that you can create work clues in a systematic and sustainable way. And that probably means letting your Post-its stay where they are for several days at a time. Clues like these work when they are used systematically and consistently, not haphazardly.

DOES THE LAYOUT OF THE OFFICE ALLOW YOU TO FLEXIBLY MOVE BETWEEN ROLES?

If juggling multiple roles is in the cards for you, you also want to look for environmental clues that you can flexibly move between roles. Some roles are so distinct that you work in different buildings depending on the day (or even hour) in which you're inhabiting that role. In academia, department chairs have a chair's office they have to sit in on chair days, even if they prefer the office in their lab space. Deans and provosts work in an entirely different building. They often feel cut off from the people in their academic departments, which creates a psychological distance as well as a pragmatic one. People who work in multiple sites—visiting different cities or even countries—are familiar with this experience.

To understand how our workspace influences our ability to move flexibly between roles, I spoke to Charlotte Priddle, a director of special collections at a university library. I met her during a special collections viewing, when she brought out Ben Denzer's *20 Slices of American Cheese*, a book made out of packaged American cheese slices. I later learned that among her many roles, by far the weirdest one is approving cheese slice orders so the book stays "fresh."

Charlotte is a librarian, the manager of a team, a hirer, a curator, and a fundraiser. Some of her roles require a lot of deep work (like strategic planning); others involve the daily grind, like creating purchase orders for cheese slices and curating the print collections.

When I asked her how she manages all these roles—many of which she bounces between on an hourly basis—she immediately brought up her physical workplace as a key enabler. Before her role was created, she worked in a siloed workplace, in which the university archives were separated from one another. There were archives for the downtown art scene, for feminist punk rock, for cuneiform tablets, and for modern manuscripts. "They were all on different floors and had different staff. They had different rules and regulations. They had their own communities," she told me.

But as someone who oversees all these different archives, it was imperative to have everyone under the same roof. A big renovation at the library made this happen, and the new space included keeping all the special collections in one place. For Charlotte, functional distance—the ability to easily move between viewing rooms and offices on a single floor—not only cut out the travel time between roles (waiting for the elevator is a hidden time suck), it also helped solidify the identity of her team. Everyone was in the same boat, dedicated to the same thing. They could see one another, literally—the library is full of glass walls—working toward that common goal.

There was an added benefit to the new, shared space that Charlotte didn't anticipate: it helped people get on board with shake-ups to the hierarchy. When she was promoted, Charlotte not only became the boss of some of her peers, but she also became her boss's boss. "The fact that *everything* changed made it easier," she told me. Not having to literally take over her boss's old office, along with the frequent, unplanned hallways conversations, helped everyone get on board with the change.

"DO I HAVE TO BE A SWAN HERE?"

Charlotte also taught me the importance of learning norms around how people communicate while juggling multiple roles. One of the most important questions she suggests you ask current employees and hirers before you take a job is "Do I need to be a swan here?"

Let me explain.

There are some workplaces that are okay with people looking flustered. If you visit an office and people are running around, hair messy and coffee stains on their clothes, they are fine with everyone seeing what it really looks like to juggle multiple things at once. The main floor of a major newspaper is like this. So, too, is an emergency department at a hospital.

And there are workplaces where the norm is for everyone to look calm and collected on the surface, but under the water their feet are beating a mile a minute to keep up, like a swan. The people might be stretched too thin, but you'd never know it by looking at their clean offices and well-pressed business attire. There might be good reasons for keeping up appearances. If the job involves interfacing with clients, for example, you don't want to look like a hot mess. It's a bit like staging your house when it's on the market. Everything is tidy when a potential buyer shows up, but an hour before the kitchen was full of dirty dishes and laundry was piled up on the floor.

Not all swan cultures should be avoided, but beware of those in which being a swan means hiding a lot of the work it takes to successfully carry out multiple roles. Those where people pretend, even to one another, that everyone is on a mission toward well-being and balance, even though they are working until midnight to complete all the hidden jobs that weren't advertised during the interview process. Where bosses and their employees can't talk bluntly about what balls have been dropped and who has time to pick them up. You want leaders to be able to say, "I'm going to drop a few balls in this role. But it's really important that you can come to me when this happens." And for people to do just that.

IS THERE A CULTURE OF "SAYING YES TO NO" HERE?

Once Charlotte learned that she would be juggling multiple roles, one of the first things she did was meet with her team to have a blunt conversation about the different ways she would inevitably tell them no.

Charlotte's nos fall into three categories: "No, I can't do that right now because we need to work out X, Y, Z." "No, that's a great idea but we don't have the funding." And "No, and I can't tell you why, because there's information I can't share with you." Anytime she said no, she backed it up with one of these explanations, so no one was left in the dark. (I would add a fourth category to your nos: "No, because I don't have the bandwidth.")

The reason why she was able to get away with her three nos is that there's a culture of saying yes to no where she works. People don't eventually get their way if they bark up enough trees, go around her to someone in power, or wear her down. Her nos were respected.

It might feel strange to ask during an interview, "Will people listen to me when I tell them no here?" Instead, ask about the culture of respecting boundaries and decisions, and whether people have alternative ways of getting their way when their boss or supervisor tells them no. In some organizations, the role-based hierarchy isn't respected as much as it should be; it's all about who you know and how long you've worked here. These are the cultures where the well-connected (or whiny) people don't take no for an answer. To the extent that their alternative methods of getting their way are reinforced, it will be very difficult for you to maintain control over the daily juggle. And as I mentioned above, many jobs come with hidden roles that you don't learn about until you've already started work. Chances are, you will be juggling more than you anticipate. You will need to have a respected "no policy" if you're going to successfully fold these roles into your workday.

Stage four: Landing the job you will love

Much of what the Stretched Too Thin career goer needs to do to land a job is similar to that of the Crisis of Identity career goer. You will need to clearly communicate your workplace identity, anchoring where you see yourself going in the role that you prioritized during your search. I suggest you read the section called "Communicate that you have a clear career identity" under stage four of the Crisis of Identity chapter, if you haven't already.

In addition to this step, you will also need to clearly communicate *how* you plan to manage multiple roles, and how you've done so in the past. And the first place to do that is in your cover letter and résumé.

EXPLAIN OVERLAPPING EMPLOYMENT DATES ON YOUR RÉSUMÉ AND COVER LETTER

One of the first things you will want to pay close attention to is the employment section of your résumé. I asked many recruiters and hirers what they look for as an indicator that someone might be "taking on too many things at once," or "stretched too thin," and I got near-perfect consensus in their answers: too many jobs or roles that overlap in the time in which you did them. If you have three jobs that all overlapped for the months of June through September 2022, that's a red flag. Same thing for the current jobs you hold that all say "—present."

Many of us think that holding three jobs at once looks impressive, but in reality, it looks like you're side hustling while currently employed, not sure of what you want to do with your life, or both.

The best way to deal with this multiple-roles-at-once problem isn't to prune them from your résumé, it's to clearly express the nature of their overlap. Most of the people who come to me with an "everywhere at once" résumé have perfectly reasonable explanations for why they had multiple roles or jobs. One role was minor and involved a once-a-month meeting (but it looked major); another was a passion role that could be reframed as skills or interests. Often, the roles are highly overlapping or integrative, but we talk about them as if they are independent to make it look like we have an even longer list of skills and accomplishments.

Embrace your multiple roles by letting them talk to one another on your résumé. If the first role involved "working with a team of twelve to increase profits by 40 percent" and your second role involved working with that same team of twelve to develop a leadership program, say so. "Worked with the same team of twelve to build out a leadership program." Integrating your roles is a skill, and hirers like to see that you know how to find overlap in the various jobs you do.

If you took on side jobs while employed, make it clear what the nature of those jobs was. There are a lot of data showing that even full-time employees are hustling on the side (and sometimes while on the clock, against their contracts). Hiring someone who's done this makes employers nervous. If you worked for two companies at once, clarify the nature of that simultaneous employment. Don't leave it to chance for résumé readers to guess.

And while you're here, make sure your LinkedIn profile page matches your résumé. Same job titles, same dates, same basic job descriptions. Many people don't get past the first stage of hiring because they have mismatches; they change how they frame their experience to match a job description on a résumé (merging two roles into one, for example), but not on their LinkedIn profile. At the early stages of sourcing candidates, recruiters typically won't confirm past employment with your employers, but they will look for consistency in how you present your work history. Lying is common on résumés when it comes to experience and education, and this is one easy way to reduce suspicion.

COMMUNICATE YOUR PLAN FOR JUGGLING MULTIPLE ROLES

Above, I taught you how to juggle multiple roles, from being strategic about your interruptions, to prioritizing one role that guides your job search. During the interview process, you will also want to communicate your prioritization plan. "Tell me how you plan to balance multiple roles" is a common request, and one that a lot of job seekers haven't thought about strategically.

There are a few skills you can showcase to answer this question. First, discuss how you plan to communicate with people at work about boundaries and prioritization. I mentioned the conversation Charlotte had with her team, when she introduced her three nos to people who came to her with a request. If you're in a position of leadership, these frank conversations go a long way toward preventing you from becoming a neglectful boss. Saying yes to everything isn't sustainable, and hirers will want to know how you will avoid this pitfall, starting with your communication plan. Mention how you plan to foster a culture of frequent feedback, so when you do drop a ball, people feel comfortable telling you about it.

Second, communicate your plan to reduce the impact of interruptions on your work. All the skills I mentioned above—from documenting your own daily interruptions, to developing an in-office plan that reduces the amount of external disruptions from your team—can be taught to others. If you're interested in creating a culture of not being stretched too thin, even better. Hirers love to see you thinking beyond yourself and your own achievements.

Third, showcase how you plan to prioritize jobs as they crop up. Charlotte comes to work every day with a two-by-two table: on one axis is urgency, on the other is importance. She places jobs into one of four quadrants based on whether urgency is high or low and importance is high or low. High-urgency but low-importance jobs get done between working spheres; these are things like purchasing cheese slices for the cheese book. High-importance, low-urgency jobs, which often involve deep thinking (like strategic planning around fundraising), get done when she has large blocks of uninterrupted time. These are the working spheres that are the most important for maintaining identity, so she protects them. Importantly, Charlotte doesn't try to piece these jobs together throughout the day. Communicate that you know how to build structures like these into your workday, giving examples of how they've been successfully implemented.

BE PREPARED TO ANSWER THE QUESTION "SHOULD YOU TAKE ON THIS ROLE, WHAT DO YOU PLAN TO GIVE UP?"

Most of us go into interviews ready to say yes to everything. But showing that you have restraint, and that you've thought carefully about what you will have to give up should you take on another role, shows an awareness that hirers will want to see.

You should already have asked yourself this question if you're in the position to take on another role. Thinking about giving things up at a high level is an important first step. Often, it's the passion roles that are first to go. But it's also important to show that you've carefully thought about the transition between roles, including things like the cost of switching between working spheres. If, for example, one of your roles requires you to work in a different physical office than the others (like the dean I mentioned earlier), what is the cost of moving between offices? If you've built little clues around your computer in one office to help you get back on track, like Post-its or notes on your wall, how are you going to bring them to the other?

I opened this chapter with Jake, the analyst who was handed a bunch of new responsibilities on top of his old ones when he absorbed his boss's jobs. The first question he should have asked his boss is this: What roles or jobs would you like me to give up, now that I'm taking on these new ones? Jake was not ready to give up his two hours of deep work a day, yet essentially that was what he was asked to do. Having a frank conversation about losses with his boss before his promotion would have saved them both a lot of trouble.

▪ ▪

TAKE-HOMES FOR EACH STAGE

STAGE ONE:

- Focus on answering two big questions: Am I taking on too many roles at work? Am I interrupted so often during the workday that I'm having a hard time getting anything done?

- If you're taking on too many roles, take stock of how much control you have in the decision, and how many roles you're taking on voluntarily.

STAGE TWO:

- Prioritize the tasks and roles you enjoy most so you can anchor your networking conversations on the role that is most closely tied to your career identity.

- Learn how to organize your work in terms of working spheres—broad categories of work that encompass multiple roles.

STAGE THREE:

- Learn what physical features of the workplace will make or break your success at pulling off multiple roles.

- Ask questions during interviews that probe the degree of autonomy you would have over scheduling your work—including whether you can stay within spheres when you work.

STAGE FOUR:

- Showcase that you have a clear identity at work, anchored on one primary role.

- During the interview, communicate your plans for executing these skills at your new job using your new skills, such as how you plan to create role overlap and reduce interruptions at work.

▪ ▪

THE RUNNER-UP

No matter how hard I try,
I can't make it to the next level up

It's been about six months since Sebastian was denied his promotion to director, and he's still simmering with rage. "I spent about two years working as a senior manager—the step below this one—and I did a pretty good job," he told me. When I ask him why he thinks he deserves the promotion, I get a well-executed speech. First comes the list of accomplishments, then the "and I'm next in line" bit. It's clear that for Sebastian, being a Runner-Up is a unique form of torture. First, he lost to Mark, who "knew the right people," then to two external hires who had his current title but worked for other organizations. He went through multiple rounds of interviews all three times, but was told, in the end, that there was someone who was just a better fit.

Like most Runners-Up, Sebastian spent a lot of time focusing on the "why not me" piece. What exactly is it about me that isn't qualified? His team performed well, and to his knowledge he hadn't burned any bridges. But he sits awake at night asking himself, "Is this due to chance—I just happened to be competing against three better people—or do I have a flaw no one has told me about?" Throughout our conversation, I can't stop thinking about a friend of mine who's desperate to get married but just can't seem to find someone who wants to go on that journey with him. There doesn't seem to be anything fundamentally wrong with him, it just hasn't worked out yet.

Like my single friend, Sebastian has spent many sleepless nights reflecting on his failures. But I was surprised to learn that he never asked himself two critical questions: How successful were these people in the roles they held *before* they became senior manager? Is it the case that they held different roles than I did before they got here? He assumed that once he was in his current role his past performance and how he got there didn't matter. That his accomplishments in this role—not in the roles he held before it—were what mattered the most. But he was wrong.

"At the time there was *no one* to take on my position," he told me, when I asked him how he got the job he holds now. The person who had it before him quit when they got long COVID, and the company was in a rush to replace them. It would have cost a ton of time and money for the organization to fill this role the traditional way: writing a job advertisement and having a recruiter interview people. So they did what many do in emergency situations like this—they hired the most motivated person in their immediate line of sight. Eager and quick to learn, Sebastian was that person.

To me, this didn't sound like a promotion dream come true, it sounded like a "battlefield promotion." Sometimes people will get promoted into a role because the organization where they work is faced with steep retention or attrition issues, and it would cost more time and money to hire externally than to promote an under-prepared person whom they plan to train. These decisions make short-term sense for organizations, but they're terrible for the pro-moted person's career. It's very hard to move up and out without holding some important middle role that other successful people have held at one point. And often when these promotions are of-fered, the person doing the hiring underplays the importance of these missed middle steps. They need someone right now, and they will do what it takes to close the deal.

For Sebastian, that middle role was first-line manager—the role in which people learned how to do things like using an "enter-prise mindset"—moving from an individual contributor who cares about their own outcomes to caring about company outcomes. They learn delegation skills and how to go from buddy to boss—the subtle art of holding power over their friends. In Sebastian's com-pany, these skills are typically learned on a team of about five to seven. In his current role, Sebastian oversees a team of thirty. In the one he's interviewing for, it's more like a team of one hundred.

Sebastian eventually learned that the people who placed him in his current role were not the same people who made the direc-tor hiring decision. This latter group was composed of a bunch of traditionalists who made it to the top taking a straight and nar-row path. They were firmly against hiring anyone who missed a step—especially one as critical as first-line manager.

But it took a good amount of detective work for Sebastian to figure this out. And truth be told, it should not have been this hard. The reasons why his company obscured the truth were not good ones; from their perspective, they wanted him to feel flattered and to say yes so they could move on to the next fire that needed to be put out. Only by networking with people outside his organization, specifically those who make hiring decisions around positions like the one he wanted, was he able to piece together the truth.

For many, promotions aren't just about looking at the success of a candidate in the role they hold right now; it's about looking at the totality of experiences accumulated along the way. And in a lot of workplaces, there are rules we must follow, even if no one told us about them. If Sebastian were to do my "Nobody told me that" exercise from the Crisis of Identity chapter, his answer would have been something like this: "Nobody told me that to make it to the role of director, you need to ignore the flattering offers of senior manager, no matter how tempting, if you haven't been a line manager first. If they tell you it's okay to miss a step, don't believe them!"

What is a Runner-Up career goer?

Not everyone who is a Runner-Up will face a problem like Sebastian did, unaware that skipping a step is what's holding them back. There are a lot of potential roadblocks out there, some of which you realize very quickly after being denied a promotion, and others that take years to discover.

But what all Runners-Up have in common is that they are experienced career goers who are having a tough time climbing up, and they often feel in the dark as to why. Out of all the career goers I cover in this book, the Runner-Up is the most certain of who they are, and the most uncertain of how they got here.

Most have been doing everything right, or at least what they thought was right, for months or years. But as I learned in doing research for this chapter, the people who make promotion decisions and those who are denied promotions diverge a lot in their beliefs about what (and sometimes who) is to blame. The goal of this chapter is to close the knowledge gap between the promotion and hiring decision-makers and the Runners-Up. The tools I give you will help you figure out the "why" part so you can move on and find a job that aligns with your future goals.

Stage one: Why am I unhappy here?

Anyone, at any career stage, can experience the frustration of not being able to land a promotion. But like Sebastian, many of us don't understand where we've gone wrong. Is it the case that we're not getting feedback from our bosses on what our shortcomings are? And if we were to ask our bosses, would they agree that they aren't giving their reports honest feedback about their shortcomings? To get to the heart of why people are in this position, I wanted to understand the nature of the communication gaps between the Runners-Up and those who promote. I would also argue that getting information from a third group of people—those who've been successfully promoted—can also provide insight into these gaps. These people might have a completely different feedback experience than the Runners-Up, having made it through the gauntlet successfully. In close relationships, we often don't agree with each other on why we broke up, or what the "real" issue is underlying a conflict. In some cases, it's because people don't clearly communicate why they're unhappy; in others, they're getting this feedback, but it's tough to take, and so they engage in all sorts of protective strategies to prevent their egos from bursting. For the Runners-Up, the first question you want to know the answer to is "Am I getting clear signals on what I've done wrong and choosing to ignore them, or do I work in a place that prioritizes nice feedback over honest and useful feedback?"

I surveyed three groups of around a hundred people each: Runners-Up (those who've failed to land a promotion that they were up for in the last six months), successfully promoted people (those who've landed a promotion they were up for in the last six months), and promotion decision-makers (those who've made a promotion decision in the last six months).

To start, I gave all three groups a list of thirteen of the most common reasons why people land, or fail to land, a promotion. For each of the thirteen reasons, I gave them four options and instructed them to select the one that best described it:

a. "I was explicitly told this by someone at work."

b. "I think this is why, but no one has said this to me."

c. "It's possible but I'm not sure."

d. "Definitely not the reason."

Here is that list. Go through it yourself, selecting one of four options above for each reason.

THIRTEEN REASONS WHY I WAS NOT PROMOTED

1. People don't respect me as much as I thought they did.

2. People don't value my contributions as much as I thought they did.

3. I thought the roles and responsibilities I hold were more important in getting a promotion than they actually are.

4. The person in charge of making promotion decisions got feedback from my team/coworkers that was negative.

5. I didn't perform well enough to earn the promotion.

6. The promotion involves leadership, and I didn't have enough leadership experience.

7. The person making the promotion decision doesn't like me.

8. The person making the promotion decision doesn't respect me.

9. The person making the promotion decision is prejudiced against me because of my group membership (e.g., my gender, race, ethnicity, social class, religion).

10. There are very few of these promotions available. They are highly competitive, and I wasn't competitive enough.

11. They didn't train me for it, so I wasn't ready for it.

12. My boss didn't have much influence over the decision of who got promoted.

13. It was close between me and another person, and the other person got it.

Among the thirteen items, how many were you able to comfortably put in option a, "I was explicitly told this by someone at work"? If you're anything like my participants, not many.

Across the thirteen items, Runners-Up on average chose "I was explicitly told this by someone at work" between 2 percent and 13 percent of the time, with an average of 7 percent! At least from their perspective, Runners-Up aren't getting feedback leading up to or following their failure to land a promotion. Knowing whether you're getting clear feedback on why you haven't succeeded is the first question you want the answer to. We need real information. It's not helpful to make up reasons or to guess.

Next, I gave this same list to promotion decision-makers. For each of the thirteen items, they were given three choices:

"People think this is why they don't get promoted, but they didn't get feedback that this is why."	"This is what people are told is the reason why they weren't promoted."	"Neither."

My goal was to get a sense of the norms of their workplace around feedback, not whether they personally delivered (or failed to deliver) feedback about why people were or weren't promoted.

Do their answers, like those of the runners-up, also reflect a lack of feedback? On average, promotion decision-makers chose "This is what people are told is the reason why they weren't promoted" about 35 percent of the time. Although decision-makers, on average, claim to work in places that give clear feedback much more frequently than Runners-Up claim to have received it (7 percent compared to 35 percent is a big gap), the data from the decision-makers are still jarring: this selection was not chosen, on average, 65 percent of the time.

Clearly decision-makers aren't giving people the feedback they need, and for some of the reasons on my list, the gap is astronomical. Take the obvious reason, "I didn't perform well enough to earn a promotion." This is the number-one reason decision-makers ostensibly tell people why they didn't get promoted (74 percent report telling people this). But Runners-Up report being told this reason 7 percent of the time.

Successfully promoted people, on the other hand, had a relatively clearer picture of what led to their promotion. I gave them the same list of thirteen items but framed them positively around their success. For example, "People don't respect me as much as I thought they did" was changed to "People respect me at work," and "People don't value my contributions as much as I thought they did" was changed to "People value my contributions." They were given the same four options as the Runners-Up, but framed in terms of why they landed the promotion. So for the successfully promoted, for each of the thirteen reasons why they were promoted, they checked one box:

a. "I was explicitly told this by someone at work."

b. "I think this is why, but no one has said this to me."

c. "It's possible but I'm not sure."

d. "Definitely not the reason why I was promoted."

Across the thirteen items, the successfully promoted chose "I was explicitly told this by someone at work" about 32 percent of the time. About 25 percent chose "It's possible but I'm not sure," and another 25 percent, "I think this is why." Like the Runners-Up, few gave alternative reasons for their promotion. The knowledge gap for why people were promoted is much smaller than the gap for why they were not, but it's still pretty big—68 percent of the time, even successful people weren't given concrete answers.

If you took the survey above and are struggling to understand why you've been unsuccessful, you're in good company. The rest of stage one is designed to help you get to the bottom of the "why" question, with an emphasis on common root causes that underlie the thirteen reasons why on my list. In relationships, when two people aren't on the same page about a fundamental issue—say, how to allocate household labor in a fair way—they often end up having conflict over small things, like why the dishes are still in the sink in the morning. These small disagreements are often symptoms of the cause rather than the cause itself. For the Runner-Up, I focus on three main root causes that cut across professions and career stages. Your goal is to get some accurate answers to these questions as you move into stage two, so you know not only your own weaknesses, but also the weaknesses of the organization that didn't promote you.

> **What are the reasons, then, really, for why I haven't been promoted?**

The reasons why people fail to land a promotion are often complex and hard to communicate. To help bring some clarity to the picture, I've distilled them to three main causes: one, the Runner-Up doesn't have an accurate perception of their status at work; two, they've experienced a "jolt" to the workplace—a sudden shift in the way work is done that disrupts team dynamics and, in turn, the status hierarchy; and three, they work in an organization that has structural roadblocks to promotion. Factors such as having a boss with little power or working in a role that doesn't have a natural "next job" are common culprits. These three things can all feed into the thirteen reasons why described above.

BIG QUESTION ONE: DO YOU KNOW HOW MUCH STATUS YOU HAVE AT WORK?

To get to the "why" piece, you will need to start by asking yourself a big question: Do I have an accurate view of my status at work?

Status is achieved by having competence and skills and having these things recognized by others around you. The first two questions on the list of thirteen reasons directly get at status: people don't respect me and value my contributions as much as I thought they did. Two other items—not having enough leadership experience and not holding the right roles and responsibilities—are also related to status. As I mentioned in the Drifted Apart chapter, many of us take on roles (often voluntarily) because we think they will give us more status. Sometimes we're wrong, which can contribute to our misperceiving our status.

Knowing how much status you have means knowing how much other people value your contributions, allow you to have influence, and defer to you because they value your opinion. It can feel a bit scary, questioning your own status at work. To get an accurate answer, you will need to ask around to make sure your perceptions are tethered to reality. Before I show you how, let's unpack what status is, and why we often get perceptions of our own status wrong.

Status is a complex thing. We perceive status (ours, and the status of others) by paying attention to how people treat one another over hundreds of interactions, often in different settings—from formal meetings in which important decisions are made, to informal chats in the hallway at work. Even small things, such as who is most likely to get a swift response to an email, can clue us in to who has status.

Despite how complicated status is, people on average are pretty accurate about where they stand relative to other people. But there's also a lot of variability around people's judgments of their own status. Some people are great at it, and others, not so much.

Why might you struggle to accurately read your own status? It turns out that sometimes status at work is based on the right things—having skills or past experiences relevant to doing their job well, or what social scientists call prestige-based status. We do things like defer to the person speaking and refrain from interrupting them when they know what they're talking about and should be listened to. If you work in an organization where status is prestige-based, then your level of competence and skill should be directly related to your status. But sometimes at work it's based on the wrong things—gender, race, and who has a nepotistic relationship with the boss are all things that grant some people status, but they aren't related to past experience or skills. Sometimes, being the loudest person in the room can give you status, even if it shouldn't.

Ask yourself: In the teams on which I work, do the people who are the most respected and have the most influence also have the most job-relevant experience or expertise?

If the answer to this question is yes, then you might need to fill in some skill gaps to improve your status. But if the answer is no, then there's a good chance that your workplace doesn't use a prestige-based model of status. The first reason why people misperceive their own status is because status isn't based on job-relevant experiences and skills where they work.

I gave the decision-makers in my study a list of fifteen status cues—some are prestige-based, and some are not—and asked them to think about what traits and behaviors characterize the people who have the most respect, admiration, and influence at their workplace (in other words, status). They were given three choices: "Definitely influence," "Does not influence," or "Not sure."

Here's that list:

- ☐ Gender
- ☐ How many people they oversee
- ☐ How smart they are
- ☐ How much they speak up in meetings
- ☐ How much they intimidate other people
- ☐ Whether they are related to another person at the company
- ☐ Whether they are friends with another person at the company
- ☐ Their ethnicity
- ☐ Their race
- ☐ Their age
- ☐ Where they went to university
- ☐ How long they've been at the company
- ☐ How much expertise they have
- ☐ How well they've performed at work
- ☐ What their job title is

Their top three answers were: one, how long they've been at the company; two, how much expertise they have; and three, how well they've performed at work (around 90 percent of decision-makers endorsed these three as "Definitely influence"). These are all prestige-based measures of status. There were, however, some traits chosen by decision-makers that have no business influencing status, including whether the person is related to another person at the company (25 percent). You want to know *before* you take a job whether decision-makers base their promotion decisions on things like nepotism, which I focus on in stage two.

It can be very difficult to get promoted if you work in a place where status isn't earned. Complete the status cue checklist above and add up how many boxes you checked off that included gender, race, ethnicity, age, whether they are related to another employee, and whether they are friends with people at work. None of these are prestige-based status cues.

The second reason why people misperceive their own status is because the cues people use to express status are often subtle and easy to miss. To pick up on these cues, you need to pay attention not only to how people respond to you, but also to how they respond to one another. You need to know, for example, that when Ashley gets interrupted by Steve it doesn't mean much; Steve interrupts everyone and he's constantly jockeying for status despite the fact that no one respects him. But when she gets interrupted by Sasha it's a big deal—Sasha is at the top of the hierarchy, and she only cuts people off when they're out of line.

Ask yourself: Do I know enough about the interpersonal dynamics among people at work to be able to figure out the status hierarchy?

You might be missing opportunities to read status cues. If status cues are expressed over emails and you're not on (or reading) all of them, you will miss them. If you work remotely or in a hybrid environment and other people are meeting in person, you will miss them. A lot of behaviors that determine status happen during informal interactions—conversations in the hallway after a meeting, for example. The more opportunities you have to observe people, the better.

The third reason why people misperceive status is that not all groups are on the same page about what should "count" as a status cue. Take, for example, age, a trait that has a lot of stereotypes associated with it. Some people think that older people with a long tenure at a company should have high status because they have more experience; others think that older people are less creative and slower at learning new things, and should have less status. Even groups that adopt a prestige-based approach to status can disagree on what skills and experiences are relevant to status. Perhaps experience matters most to one team; where you went to university, to another.

Ask yourself: Does my team spend more time jockeying for status and trying to decide whose voice should matter than doing actual work?

If the answer is yes, you probably belong to a group that spends a lot of time on what scientists call the status conferral process—trying to figure out who should have a lot of status and who should have very little. These groups lack the consensus they need to decide what matters for status and what doesn't.

WHAT DOES ACCURACY IN READING THE STATUS HIERARCHY AT WORK HAVE TO DO WITH GETTING A PROMOTION?

The costliest mistake you can make is falsely believing you have more status than you do. But it turns out being inaccurate in any direction can make it tough for you to land a promotion at work.

Why?

People who know how much status they have are also good at knowing how much status other people have. And this knowledge is critical when it comes to knowing whom to network with *outside* your own work groups. Business school professors Siyu Yu and Gavin Kilduff found that when we connect with the right people at work—those who can give us insider information, like whom to go to for help—we perform better. For example, imagine that you want to create a new initiative at work, but you don't know what strategies will be the most effective at convincing your team to side with you. High-status others will teach you tricks of the trade, like whether proposing a quid pro quo is your best bet. The people who take the advice of these high-status people perform well, which in this example means convincing the team to side with them.

There's another benefit to knowing the status hierarchy, which I'll dive into more in the next section: it helps you know how much influence your boss or manager has over who gets promoted. One of the structural reasons why you might be struggling to get promoted has nothing to do with your status or performance; it has to do with your boss's. People who know this seek out alternative paths to promotions. They network with bosses who do have persuasive power, or they ask to switch teams to work with these bosses.

SO I MIGHT NOT BE GREAT AT READING MY STATUS. WHAT SHOULD I DO?

There's a lot that goes into reading status at work. But even if your judgments are off, there are small steps you can take to increase the accuracy of your perceptions.

The first goal is to figure out how to read status cues. As I mentioned above, these are often subtle, but you can start with something simple. Over the course of several meetings or team interactions, jot down your observations about one thing: When someone speaks, do others follow up their comments and reference the person, or do they switch gears completely?

Imagine, for example, that there's someone named Jace on your team. When Jace makes a comment ("I really think that we should cut our operating budget in half this year"), do people follow up by referencing Jace ("I agree with what Jace just said, but I would add that . . .")? Or is there a pause and then a shift in topic? If there's a long pause after Jace speaks, followed by Tracy stepping in and saying, "I wanted to talk about the recruiting strategy, if that's okay with everyone," then Jace's comment fell flat. Low-status people often don't have influence because they can't get their ideas to stick with the team. Especially in overly nice cultures where people feel rude interrupting each other, status cues often take the form of lulls or breaks in a conversation following something a low-status person said.

Ask yourself: When you speak up, do people follow up your question directly and reference you, or is there a shift in topic?

Second, learn how to ask around. After you've collected some data, test your assumptions about status with your boss or manager or a leader on your team. Don't ask, "Do I have status here?" (It's vague, it's rude to say no, and they might not know.) Instead ask, "Do you think my contributions during our discussion about budget cuts made much of an impact?" And if not, ask why. Ask about the components that go into status—do people respect my opinions, do I have influence, is there someone else with more experience people tend to defer to—but not about status itself.

Third, learn who has status outside your team but within your organization. One of the benefits of working in person is that people get the lay of the land when it comes to knowing whom to go to for help, and what makes the boss tick. Remote workers need to ask explicit questions about these things to figure out who the informal leaders are at work. These "out-of-team" network connections are key to climbing up, even if you're low in status to begin with. Work on forming these connections before you leave a job. You might be failing to get a promotion because you're going to the wrong people for advice—people you think have more respect and influence than they actually do.

BIG QUESTION TWO: DID YOU EXPERIENCE A JOLT IN THE WORKPLACE?

Sometimes at work we fail to get promoted because fate has intervened and completely disrupted the status hierarchy at work. One day we had status, the next day it's gone. Jolts are organizational-level changes that have two key features: one, they're highly disruptive, requiring employees to support one another so they can manage the glitches that come along with the change; and two, they shake up the status hierarchy. Going from working in an office to working from home is a jolt most of us have experience with. The factors that helped us maintain our status pre-jolt (like sitting at the front of the room) were no longer effective post-jolt (there is no front seat on Zoom). About a quarter of the Runners-Up in my study experienced a jolt—a third of successfully promoted people and half of bosses. Jolts are common.

Jolts can feel sudden, and you might be caught completely off guard if one happens to you. Imagine, for example, that your company, located in a bilingual nation, changed its official language to English. Starting the next day, all company meetings must be held in English. Instantly, the non-native English speakers would feel a drop in status. As another example, imagine a sudden introduction of new technology that everyone has to use. The next day, all the "techies" would feel an increase in status. Many of the company-wide changes that I talk about in the Drifted Apart chapter would be considered jolts.

Elijah Wee at the University of Washington and his coauthors studied how jolts influence how people deal with potential status drops. They focused on teams at a real estate firm in Southeast Asia that experienced a jolt in the types of homes they would be selling (they shifted from the private sector to the public sector). Importantly, everyone experienced the jolt, but the vice president sent out an email to half the teams telling them that they would need to start over and build a new list of contacts following the jolt. The other half weren't told this. The framing of the jolt had a huge impact on how people behaved.

People with status coming into the jolt—those who had a lot of contacts (which is gold in real estate) were so threatened by the jolt that they sabotaged themselves by doing things like hoarding resources and insider tips. Employees with little status going into the jolt viewed it as an opportunity to climb up. They acted like team players, sharing resources and insider tips. In fact, many of these previously low-status people surpassed their higher-status team members, post-jolt.

If you've experienced a jolt at work—like 24 percent of the Runners-Up in my study did—you might have been knocked down a level or two on the status hierarchy. If you have a lot of status pre-jolt, be mindful that you're not shooting yourself in the foot by doing things like refusing to share resources with colleagues whom you view as competitors, even if you feel like that will lead to short-term gains. Runners-Up with all the markers of status might be wondering, "What on earth did I do wrong?" The answer might be something as simple as "You acted purely in your own self-interest. And nobody likes that." If you experience a jolt at work, act fast. Carefully read the situation and change course if your prior status-seeking behaviors no longer help you get respect and admiration from other people. Your goal is to keep yourself on track to get a promotion, and being adaptable to jolts is key to achieving that goal.

BIG QUESTION THREE: ARE THERE STRUCTURAL ROADBLOCKS TO PROMOTION WHERE YOU WORK?

In this stage, I've focused so far on what you might be doing wrong, but sometimes there are barriers to your success that are outside your control; structural features of the workplace that are hidden from view until you try to climb up and realize you can't.

People don't usually think of their boss as one of those barriers. But one of the most common reasons why people fail to get promoted is because their boss doesn't have as much influence as they think they do. Obviously having a boss who wants to promote you is essential. But what about one who does believe in you, but just doesn't have the power to make it happen?

I spoke with Subbu Kalpathi, an engineer by training and an author, who has also been a teacher, public speaker, computer engineer, and consultant. He's worked for start-ups with a handful of employees and huge organizations with thousands of employees. One of the lessons he's learned is that sometimes even a well-intentioned boss can't do much to close the deal for you. Either they aren't respected enough, they haven't been working at the company long enough to have influence, or it's not "their turn" to pick the next promotion.

In one of his jobs, Subbu realized after a failed promotion that he was up against a hundred other people who all worked at the company. His boss, who was new, learned at the promotion decision meeting that people in Subbu's position need to be working for at least a year before they're eligible. It didn't matter how well someone's direct report performed, tenure at the company was the critical status dimension they used for prioritizing promotion requests.

Ask yourself: Does my boss have as much influence as I think they do?

Status can work like an invisible string yoking you to your boss. If they don't have it, neither will you. But don't expect your boss to tell you this; in my survey of decision-makers, only 16 percent reported that at their workplace it was clearly communicated to people who failed a promotion that their boss "doesn't have much influence over who, among the people they competed with, got promoted."

You can learn the status of your boss the same way you learn about your own status—networking, observing behaviors between people, and marking down things like whether their perspectives, when shared, influence decisions. Indirect methods are better, as people are rarely willing to admit their own status shortcomings. And when you network, keep track of which bosses were tied to promotions, not just which people were promoted.

Bosses who are well connected will also help you get to the bottom of a very important question: whether there is a real "next job" for you at this organization. At your workplace, the next-step job might be so far removed from what you do now that it wouldn't be a promotion, it would be a career pivot.

Ask yourself: Does this organization where I work have a role that is the natural next step for me?

I met Zoe, a head of sales in the west for a U.S.-based company, who experienced this roadblock recently. Zoe is a fantastic team leader. So good, in fact, that her team brought in 80 percent of the revenue for the region. With the numbers to back her, she was itching to get promoted to a VP role. But the problem was, the VP role involved overseeing a huge region in the United States—a much bigger area than she was used to, and one in which she had no contacts (in sales, it's all about the contacts).

Frustrated at the lack of promotion opportunity, Zoe and a few other top sales leaders did some digging. They realized that they were facing a hidden barrier no one had told them about: To do well at their current job, they needed to form a network of potential customers that was deep but not wide—it contained a lot of close relationships with people in a relatively small region. But to land a promotion, they needed the opposite—a network that was wide but not deep; they would have to know a lot of people across the United States, but they didn't need to have developed relationships with many of them. The VP would instruct their team to develop deep relationships within their region.

It turned out that because of this barrier, no one in her role had ever been promoted to VP. Most stayed where they were, happy to take a big commission. Instead, VP positions were filled by external hires—people who held VP roles in competitive companies and had the networks to show for it. Her boss, who hadn't been part of any promotion decisions (she was six months on the job), didn't know this.

If most people who hold your aspirational role aren't hired internally but externally, you might be confronting a structural barrier like Zoe did. In stage three you will want to ask specific questions that get at these barriers. How many people who hold your aspirational role held another role at this organization, and how long did it take them to climb up? Are the skills needed to succeed at this job related to the ones needed to succeed at the one below it, or are they different in kind?

Stage two: What do I want my future career to look like?

By the end of stage one, you will have started to uncover what is holding you back at work: you will be learning how much status you have, if there are gaps in your skills or past experiences, if you have experienced a jolt, and whether are there structural barriers, including a low-status boss, that are holding you back. It's okay if you don't have all the reasons worked out yet. In stage two, you'll continue exploring these questions with the help of your network connections.

As I mentioned in the Crisis of Identity and Stretched Too Thin chapters, most well-established career goers have a lot of network connections within their company and their industry. Runners-Up typically fall into this category too. The networking strategy for stage two involves talking to people who oversee the role you want and who've either held it in the past or hold it now.

The mistakes that Runners-Up make start long before they try to get a promotion, and often when they take a job that is two or three steps before it. Missteps may start at the job-seeking stage, when we fail to ask the right questions about promotion opportunities. The questions below are meant to be asked early, before you're ready to apply. As you go through this stage, target people who work for different organizations. Local company-based norms are strong, and as I've mentioned throughout this book, your goal is to look for themes in people's answers that cut across where they work.

The key to success here is basing your networking strategy around the role you want, not the company you want to work for. Runners-Up have grass-is-greener problems; they often fall in love with an organization where they think their path to success would be easier than it is where they are now. It's often not, so to prevent that bias from kicking in, think broadly about your connections.

WILL I NEED TO FILL IN ROLES YOU MISSED TO BE COMPETITIVE?

Sebastian, the person I opened this chapter with, underestimated the degree to which holding a first-line manager role was a necessary step for his climb up. Some professions have roles that are must-haves in the sense that they are the only way to get a certain type of experience. But clearly not everyone agrees on how must-have these roles really are, or the Sebastians of the world would have heard about them. Instead, the importance of these roles varies from organization to organization. They can even vary locally, from team to team. For example, in my department at NYU, we have two areas within the department of psychology. In one area (cognition) there is a strong norm only to hire faculty who have held a postdoctoral position before becoming a faculty member— a "middle-step" role in academia. In another area (social psychology), there's a norm to hire people right out of graduate school. The difference in training between these two options is one to four years. But once here, they are treated equally and given the same job title, salary, and expectations for performance (despite the training difference).

When you connect with people in your professional network, ask them to tell you about their work histories. You're looking for themes around what roles everyone who's been promoted held at some point, even if no one is really talking about why these roles are important. As is the case with jargon usage and other forms of normative behavior, there might be an implicit "everybody knows that" understanding around the importance of holding these roles. You might not know how important they are. And as with jargon and norms in general, the only way to learn is to ask.

HAVE YOU ASSUMED THAT THE ROLES YOU'VE TAKEN ON ARE MORE "UP AND OUT" THAN THEY ACTUALLY ARE?

In the chapter on the Stretched Too Thin career goer, I introduced you to three categories that roles fall into: day-to-day, up-and-out, and passion roles. Day-to-day roles take up the most time and get at the heart of your work. They are often the ones most tightly related to performance. If you don't master these it will be tough to get promoted at work. Up-and-out roles help you move beyond your current position. These roles give you visibility and showcase skills that differ from the day-to-day ones. The best versions of these are leadership roles outside your immediate domain (you chaired a committee on strategic planning). Passion roles are the ones you love—they give your work meaning, but they probably don't give you status. Only the luckiest among us can climb up at work through our passion roles.

Write out the roles you have at work and put them into these three categories. When you talk to your network connections, test your assumptions about your categorizations. For example, are you taking on too many day-to-day roles that aren't necessary for promotion? Runners-Up sometimes fall into a diminishing-returns trap; the amount of effort it takes to continue doing these roles isn't tethered to the benefits they get from performing well. At one point these roles were important, but not anymore. For me, that means publishing chapters in someone else's book (which is very different from publishing a book of your own). They do little for me at this stage in my career, but they were much more important early in my career when I didn't have many publications. It took me awhile to update my thinking about their importance.

A much bigger mistake Runners-Up make is incorrectly categorizing their up-and-out roles. As I discussed in stage one, it can be very difficult to accurately gauge your own status at work, and one reason why you might be struggling is because you assume that the roles that make you visible at work—the ones that give you an opportunity to meet senior leaders or be invited to important meetings—also gain you respect. But that's not always the case.

Here's an example.

I spoke to a chief human resources officer who told me about a recent problem at her workplace. There's a trend for people to start their own employee resource group (ERG), which is designed to bring people together who have a shared identity and who might otherwise have a hard time connecting with one another. Recently, the CEO has decided to be more involved in diversity and inclusion issues, so once a month, she meets with all the chairs of the ERGs so they can share the needs of their groups. Many of these chairs see this as a golden opportunity to press the flesh of the CEO. The problem is, the meetings centered around ERGs don't showcase the skills CEOs typically care about for promotion decisions. People are volunteering in droves to start their own ERGs because they mistake these passion roles for up-and-out roles.

Be careful that you aren't mislabeling your up-and-out roles. About 20 percent of the Runners-Up in my study have taken on a role because it helped their reputation; 10 percent did it because they believed it impressed the person who asked them to do it; and another 11 percent because they think it impresses someone in power. But among these same participants, over a quarter of them (26 percent) thought the reason they didn't get a promotion was because they believed their roles and responsibilities were more important than they are, despite no one explicitly telling them this.

Ask your network connections, "I have been doing this role for a while now, but I'm not sure it's helping me advance my career. In what ways do you think role is relevant (or not) to my goals?" In the case of the ERG people, the answer would be "It's great that you're doing this and you get to meet the CEO. But she doesn't leave those meetings with any sense of your performance at work, just your passion about your group." A simple question with a simple answer can save you loads of time and energy on a role that is not helping you get where you want to be.

DO YOU HAVE A GOOD SENSE OF HOW SCARCE THIS ROLE IS?

Opportunities shrink at the top, and when it comes to big promotions, many of us have our base rates wrong. We base our knowledge on things like how many job postings there are for the role, or how many people in our social networks hold the role now or have held it in the past.

About 55 percent of bosses in my study report explicitly telling someone whom they didn't promote that there are few of these positions available, and they weren't competitive enough. But only 10 percent of Runners-Up report being told this exact reason for not being promoted. Either leaders are terrible at communicating scarcity, or Runners-Up aren't fully understanding what scarcity means when it's communicated to them.

Probably both are true. But there's a lot of ways in which our perceptions of scarcity might be off.

One, most of us think locally about competition. Who in our own workplace is the most relevant social comparison for the promotion we want? Perhaps it's John, in the cubicle next to you. John always seems to be doing a little bit better than you, and it irks you, so you constantly monitor him. John might be up for your promotion, but in reality, John is probably only one of hundreds of people in the pool. I see this a lot in academia. Students compare themselves to other students in their program: Who has

more papers? Who gives a better presentation? But the real competition is a sea of nameless people they don't know anything
about.

About half of Runners-Up thought they knew everyone they
were competing against for a promotion (55 percent). Most also
thought they lost out to someone at their own workplace (67 percent). Given the huge communication gaps between Runners-Up
and decision-makers, who knows how tethered to reality these
numbers are? Competition for promotions is a black box.

Two, we rarely learn about how many people are in an applicant pool. Recruiters and hiring managers don't typically give this
information to candidates ("You're competing against fifty other
people for this job"). One reason why is that these numbers are
constantly changing; they can't give you an honest answer, even if
they wanted to. As I've discussed throughout the book, the hiring process is often iterative—the job opens, candidates apply, it
closes then opens again, new candidates apply. There's not a static
number of people in the pool. Another reason is that many jobs
are filled without ever being advertised, so the "pool of applicants"
is a theoretical one, not a real one. Getting the job comes down
to who you know, not how many résumés were submitted into a
portal.

At this stage, it's important to know if you're chasing a role
that, probabilistically, is unlikely to land in your lap. The best way
to get an accurate understanding of your chances is to speak to
people who hire for your role. Start by asking how many people,
relative to those who are competitive, get this role per year (or

quarter). The key here is "relative to those who are competitive." It's not useful to know that a thousand people applied for a job if only five have the qualifications for it. But if only 5 percent of highly competitive people get a role, then your chances are obviously slim, even if you're one of them. Next, ask them, "What needs to happen for the role to open up?" In many workplaces, there are hidden barriers to roles—budgets are cut, someone needs to retire, someone needs to get fired. In other workplaces, they post about ten offers for the role per year pretty systematically.

Stage three: Go on a fact-finding mission to test whether a career is a good fit for you

By the time you finish working through stages one and two, you should know what steps you need to take to improve the chances of landing a promotion at your next job—whether that is filling in gaps in your résumé by taking on additional middle-step roles, or shifting gears, dropping roles that are less up-and-out than you originally thought they were. You might learn that you need to work for a bit longer at your current job or in a role adjacent to yours before you're competitive for a promotion.

Stage three is for people who are ready to leave their current job, either for that next step or to make a parallel move. Below I cover main questions that you want to ask hiring managers, interviewers, and recruiters during this process. But first, here are two general pieces of advice.

DON'T ANCHOR YOUR SEARCH ON JOB TITLES

Most of the Runners-Up in my study are looking for a title change—around 83 percent. Title changes are markers of status, so I understand the temptation to want one. But there's a lot that can go wrong with anchoring your search on a title change. There used to be a shared understanding of what titles meant for different industries, but not anymore. New ones are invented all the time. For example, before the pandemic, listings with the title "senior" in them hovered around 3.9 percent; as of spring 2022, they doubled to 6.2 percent. The creators of jobs and job ads have quickly figured out that they can draw more people to apply with lofty-sounding job titles than accurate ones.

If you're tempted to apply for a job because it has a title with "senior" or "C-whatever" in it (like Chief Happiness Officer), get to the bottom of what the job entails to see what's substantively behind it. And critically, ask people outside the company hiring if they've ever heard of that title and what they think it means. A fancy title won't help you gain status at work if no one outside a small inner circle respects it.

COME PREPARED TO INTERVIEW WITH A SPECIFIC LIST OF CHANGES YOU MIGHT ENCOUNTER, GOOD AND BAD, SHOULD YOU TAKE THIS JOB

Many of us are so excited at the opportunity to take on a job with promotion potential that we spend the whole interview either trying to impress or asking about future opportunities—good things that might come our way if we play our cards right. But usually, promotions are a mixed bag. With more responsibility comes more stress, a higher workload, and probably less work-life balance. In the Stretched Too Thin chapter, I advise you to ask during the interview, "Is there a culture of 'saying yes to no' here?" That advice applies here too. Promotions often involve juggling multiple roles, and you want to be careful you don't turn into a Stretched Too Thin person, taking on so many new things to impress your boss that you wind up doing everything at once, and therefore nothing at all.

I gave the Runners-Up and the successfully promoted people in my study a list of thirteen factors that might change if they got the promotion they wanted (for the Runners-Up), or did change following a promotion (for the successfully promoted). For each item, they reported whether they would have (or had) "more," "less," "the same," or "I don't know" of each factor. That list is below.

THE CHANGE LIST

1. Compensation

2. Amount of responsibility

3. Number of people I oversee

4. Leadership responsibilities

5. Flexibility in work hours

6. Amount of travel

7. Respect from coworkers

8. Stress

9. Work-life balance

10. Say over my schedule

11. Say over my working hours

12. Say over where I work

13. Influence over decisions

Take this quiz yourself. How optimistic are you that should you land your promotion, you'll get more of the good things and less of the bad?

Here's what I found in my data.

On average, Runners-Up think they would have "more" of everything that falls into the status-enhancing category—about 80 percent more responsibility, compensation, leadership, respect from coworkers, and influence over decisions. These numbers align with the experiences of the successfully promoted, who averaged about 78 percent in the "more" category across these things following their promotions.

Where the two groups diverge is the psychological toll that the promotion takes. Around 68 percent of the successfully promoted experience more stress after their promotion, compared to around 60 percent of Runners-Up who anticipate experiencing more stress. About 15 percent of the successfully promoted have more work-life balance following a promotion, compared to 25 percent of Runners-Up who anticipate having more work-life balance. When we forecast into the future, we tend to overestimate the degree to which things will get better for us and underestimate the degree to which they will get worse.

Bring this list to your late-stage interviews—once you've learned about a role and are close to taking it. Ask to speak with people who hold the role you're aspiring toward and give them my checklist. Your goal is to give yourself a reality check around what your future role will look like. And remember the results of your Daily Stress Test, which I introduced in the opening of this book. If people tell you that stress has gone up since their promotion, probe into what the day-to-day of the job looks like to understand why. You want to make sure your goals for your promoted job align with your psychological needs.

THE INTERVIEW

In this chapter, I presented a lot of data on communication gaps between decision-makers who grant promotions and the people who seek them out. Approach interviews with the hypothesis that you are more likely not to know what's going on behind the scenes when it comes to promotion decisions than you are to know. Treat the interview as an opportunity to find evidence that disproves this hypothesis. To guide you, here's a list of probing questions.

Is there a protocol for sourcing and reviewing applicants that you can tell me about?

I recommend various forms of this question throughout this book. For Runners-Up, the goal is to get some clarity around the "competition black box" I mentioned in stage two—the idea that many Runners-Up don't know how scarce a role is. You might land this job now, but asking this question will give you insight into the likelihood of getting a promotion at this company in the future. Specific questions like "Do you have decision-making rules around who is eligible for promotions, such as tenure at the company?" showcase that you're thinking long term. And ones like "Do you have prioritization rules around which managers can promote someone, or is everyone who is eligible put into the same pool to be considered, regardless of who their manager is?" are important if you're thinking about becoming a manager one day (and knowing how the status of your manager will matter for your future).

Companies should be able to tell you what their processes are for hiring and promotion. At my job, I've run many faculty searches. We have a protocol, and I'm happy to share it with anyone who asks. There are also rules around who is eligible for promotion to tenure (anyone who has been working there for five years must go up), and full professor (you can choose never to go up, but at minimum you need to hold the role of associate professor for five years, with a few exceptions). These things should not be treated as company secrets. Without clear processes in place, there are a lot of opportunities for biases to impact promotion decisions. Traits like gender, race, and whether you're related to the boss (things that are not the prestige-based status cues I discussed in stage one) can influence who gets promoted. I discussed how these traits can influence who has status in teams, but they can also influence who makes it onto a team.

What is the feedback process like following a promotion failure and a promotion success?

Ask very specific questions about the feedback process throughout the interview, including after failures. Ask how managers and bosses deliver the feedback, when, and what the structure of that feedback is. Answers like "If you didn't make the cut, we expect your manager to tell you why" are red flags. If those managers aren't held accountable for delivering feedback, or there aren't guidelines to make sure the feedback is specific and useful, you're leaving a lot up to chance.

Are the skills I need for the next step a natural extension of the skills I needed to succeed in this role, or are they different in kind?

Many people are promoted without the skills they need to succeed in their new role. In this case, a promotion isn't an opportunity, it's a jolt—a huge change to the workplace, in which there are new rules for how to succeed, and the status you had coming into the role is no longer relevant. Because their skills (or network connections) aren't as useful in their new role as they were in their old one, people in this situation not only face an uphill battle when it comes to performing, but also have a hard time holding onto status at work. As a consequence, many turn to micromanagement. When you don't know what to do in your new role, you overmanage the people who hold your old one.

Naturally, there will be new skills you need to have once promoted. But none of these skills should come as a surprise on day one of your new job. Your organization needs to set up the process of skills building *before* they promote you, not after. They should have a process of identifying people who have promotion potential early and start preparing them. For you, this can mean shadowing people in your future role or taking training courses that the company builds into your workday. Whatever that process is, the interviewer should be able to tell you about it during the interview.

Can I set up a succession plan before I leave my current role?

As a natural extension of the question above, ask whether there is a succession plan in place, once they leave their current role. The handful of Runners-Up in my study who provided additional reasons for not getting promoted mentioned things like "I'm too expensive to replace" or "There is no one to do my current job if I'm promoted out of it." If you're good at your job, you might be failing to climb up because it's too costly to replace you. And sometimes that cost isn't immediately apparent. Imagine, for example, that you work in sales, and you currently manage a team of five, all of whom bring in $20,000 a year in sales. It might be much more difficult for the company to replace you—someone who knows how to train a team of people to bring in revenue—than it is to replace an individual contributor who brings in $100,000 a year in sales on their own. The financial bottom line is the same, but the skills needed to get there are different.

Look for red flags that people are too good, too expensive, or too inconvenient to replace. You don't want to take a role that is too precious. These roles are often the reason people feel like Underappreciated Stars—the topic of the next chapter.

Stage four: Landing the job you will love

For the Runner-Up, a big part of landing the job is showing that you've thought carefully about the decision-making rules around promotions and around potential roadblocks you might face, and that you're not just chasing titles or anchoring your search to the perks of the job.

When I asked decision-makers in my study what changes their promotion decisions involve, about 31 percent reported handling promotions that involve "completely different responsibilities than the ones the person has now." One person wrote about how a promotion involved going from analyzing data to accessing the company funds and being involved in trading operations. Another wrote about how the person would go from being a draftsperson in the field to an architectural technologist involved in technical design decisions.

For this reason, the section on landing the job for the Stretched Too Thin career goer is also relevant here. Much of that advice, like communicating your plan for juggling multiple roles and being prepared to answer the question "Should you take on this role, what do you plan to give up?" is also appropriate for the Runner-Up. So, too, is the advice I give on making sure your different roles at work are integrated and "talk to one another" on your résumé. Promoters need to see that you're taking systematic steps in your career, not just bouncing from one thing to another.

In addition, below are three pieces of advice to keep in mind during the interview process.

HEDGE APPROPRIATELY WHEN ASKED ABOUT YOUR PREPARATION FOR A ROLE

Throughout this book I've advised you to not oversell your skills and experiences, and to make it clear what you're ready to do and what you will need some more guidance with. Runners-Up often want to impress interviewers with their list of accomplishments, but hedging appropriately also shows restraint. When you interview, you want to say things like "In general I feel prepared to take on the role of technical design decisions, because I've done X and Y in the past to prepare me. However, when it comes to the specific task of Z, I would love some additional training. Can you tell me about that opportunity?" This is especially the case if you're in that 30 percent of people who, following a promotion, will be handed roles that are completely different from the ones you have now. No one expects you to know how to do everything. Interviewers are looking for self-insight into what you're comfortable asking for help with.

SHOW THAT YOU'VE DONE YOUR "WHERE I WANT TO GO" RESEARCH FOR THE SPECIFIC COMPANY YOU'RE INTERVIEWING FOR

I was recently giving career advice to someone who had carefully crafted a cover letter and résumé around where he wanted to see his career going. He did a great job showing how his contributions to company-level outcomes made him well suited to train other people to do the same. The "return on investment" section of his letter was great; it highlighted the financial bottom line of his successes.

He had landed an interview, and he wanted some help preparing. I asked him some specifics about the company he was interviewing for, a boutique firm in Europe. "How many employees do they have, and among those, how many have been at the company since it was created ten years ago?" I asked.

He looked puzzled. He'd spent a lot of time focusing on how to frame his successes, but he'd completely forgotten to go onto LinkedIn, find out who works for the company, and dig into their job histories. He didn't know how many (among the thirty or so employees) had been promoted from within, and how many showed up one day and were handed a C-suite title.

It seems obvious that you should do your research into the

specific company you're interviewing for, but Runners-Up can be so focused on convincing the interviewer they can handle a promotion that they don't practice perspective-taking, and they forget to find out what other people's paths to success have been in the past. That research can start with a quick glance at the company's website or their LinkedIn page. Small insights like "I noticed that about half of the people who currently work here have been promoted from within, based on changing titles in their profiles. That's great! It sounds like you have a great promotion trajectory here" show that you've done your homework. Companies want to promote people who show investment in them in particular. And that investment starts with putting time into learning about the company.

It's like going on a date and mentioning small details about the person that you learned from the friend who set you up, or from their dating profile. You don't want to talk about yourself the whole time. You want to say things like "I heard you lived in Hong Kong for two years. That sounds cool!" It shows interest. And just like dating, small details work great. You don't need to have memorized everything about the company.

THINK ABOUT HOW TO FRAME A PARALLEL OR STEP-DOWN MOVE, IF YOU'RE MAKING ONE

At one point in his career, Subbu was so burned out in his role that he decided to switch jobs to take on something that came with less responsibility. The company he had been working for was a start-up, and he was spread too thin, taking on the roles of a dozen people at once. He had been promoted to a high-up position in the start-up, but the stress wasn't worth it.

So he decided that to get the role he really wanted, he would need to take a step down to take a step up. No more start-ups, only well-established companies. But the problem was, he was so seasoned and successful that none of these companies were convinced he would actually stick around in a lower-status role.

After you've gone through stages one and two, you might realize that to get promoted, you will have to fill in lost roles. Or like Subbu, you might realize that the status of the role matters less than the type of company you want to work for and the kind of work you want to do. Subbu had to convince this company, which sat on making a decision about him for several weeks, that he wasn't going to leave the minute a better opportunity opened up. And a lot of that convincing came down to walking through what his trajectory at this company would look like. He communicated his plan for climbing up and asked for feedback about his timelines to make sure it was tethered to reality.

Runners-Up often don't think that part of being successful at a promotion is convincing a hirer that you will stay in a role that has less status than the one you have now. You want to communicate that you're not taking a role out of desperation or because the market is thin. Statements like "I realize that this role comes with less decision-making power, and a lower compensation than what I have now. But I've thought long term about the utility of this role. My plan is to build into the role of X after I've mastered the skills of Y, which I don't yet have" will ease the concerns of interviewers.

■ ■

TAKE-HOMES FOR EACH STAGE

STAGE ONE:

■ Runners-Up often don't get clear, consistent feedback on what they're doing wrong; even the people who hire and fire report that this feedback is infrequent.

■ Get answers to three big questions: One, do I know how much status I have at work? Two, did I experience a jolt in the workplace (a sudden shift in who has status and who does not)? And three, are there structural roadblocks to promotion where I work?

STAGE TWO:

■ Use your network connections to answer the question "Do I need to fill in roles that I missed to be competitive?"

■ Learn how scarce a role is by asking how many people who are competitive for that role ultimately get it.

STAGE THREE:

■ When job hunting, don't anchor your search on job titles.

■ Create a list of changes you might encounter following a promotion (good and bad), so you can analyze and are prepared for not only what might improve in your life, but also what might get worse (like your well-being).

■ Use the interview process to get clarity around roadblocks you might face on your road to promotion in a new organization. Ask: What is the feedback process following a failure? Are there steps in place to setting up a succession plan should I leave my current role?

STAGE FOUR:

■ Show restraint during the interview by communicating not only what you can do now, but what you would like training on.

■ Come prepared with knowledge about the company you're interviewing with. Small things, like knowing how many of their executives were promoted from within, showcase your commitment to the organization.

■ ■

THE UNDERAPPRECIATED STAR

I'm underpaid and undervalued compared to what I bring to the workplace

When I sat down to write this final chapter, I struggled with how to begin it. Who, among all the people I interviewed, perfectly captured the Underappreciated Star? Should it be the accomplished biologist David, who's been doing cutting-edge research for twenty years despite not seeing more than an inflation pay raise for a decade? Or the chief financial officer Christine, the office glue who spends just as much time mitigating conflict between her boss and the team as she spends on the job she was hired to do?

It's tough to choose among the stars I've met and chatted with, largely because most of them had a hard time with the "star" label. I got a lot of "You want to interview me for *what* chapter?" "Oh, that's not me. Who would call themselves that?"

Calling yourself an Underappreciated Star does take a certain amount of bravado—not everyone's into the "star" part, although most were fine with the "underappreciated" part. But the bigger problem I faced was convincing top performers that they were in fact stars, and underappreciated. Even the ones who hadn't seen a real raise in decades—who were rewarded for their hard work with more work—hedged a bit when I suggested that they were both of these things.

Many people who fall into this category don't realize how special their skills are—that they are "stars." Often the skills they hold are undervalued in the market for their profession. Very few engineers, for example, are hired for the soft skill of being good at conflict resolution. But those who are good at it have an enormous impact on things like turnover and engagement. This skill is rarely measured or documented, in part because it's hard to capture and in part because its effects on performance are often indirect.

Other people know the worth of their skills (and so do their bosses), but the skills are so bespoke that if they moved up in the organization there would be no one to replace them. The organization both values them and puts them in a corner.

And then there are the people who are so used to being underappreciated they've forgotten what it feels like not to be. They're like a spouse who has been doing all the household labor for so long, they can't even imagine what it would be like to come home to find dinner on the table. Many people who fall into this category are numb to the disproportionate amount of work they've been doing relative to others, often for years.

The other categories of career goers in this book can figure out, with some self-work, what category they fall into—whether they are having a true Crisis of Identity and want to switch careers, feel Stretched Too Thin because they have too many roles, or have Drifted Apart from their job because it's changed in ways that have made it unrecognizable. The potential Underappreciated Star needs to dig a bit deeper before they're ready for stage one. Embracing the label is its own form of self-work. To help get you started, let's start with some clear definitions.

What is an Underappreciated Star, and how do I know if it's me?

First, let's start with the word "star."

In the last chapter on the Runner-Up, I schooled you on the importance of learning about status at work. What it is, why it's important to know how much you have, and how to get more of it. One reason why people are reluctant to embrace the "star" part of the Underappreciated Star is because they aren't at the top of the status hierarchy at work. They aren't in the C-suite, they don't make the most money, and they don't have the fanciest office. And they certainly aren't granted all the respect and admiration by others. People don't always defer to them (even if they should) or ask their opinions in meetings.

Having status at work is not a criterion for labeling yourself a star in this book. Stars come in many shapes and forms, and many don't have much status at all (hence the underappreciated part). Many work in organizations that don't use a prestige-based model of granting status; in these organizations, people care more about things like family connections to the boss or going to a fancy private school than they do about having skills relevant to the job.

In my view, a workplace star has three components: One, you have a skill that is relevant to the workplace. This skill, when executed, either directly impacts performance (you're a basketball player who makes three-pointers) or indirectly impacts it (you translate your boss's garbled emails into clear instructions for your team). Two, that skill is rare at work; not everyone has it. If everyone on the basketball team makes three-pointers, or everyone knows what the boss really means in those emails, your skill is not rare. Three, you are better at this skill than other people at work. Your three-pointer average is higher. The other people who try to translate the bad emails get it half right. You always get it totally right.

The third criterion is arguably the hardest to evaluate, and one of the biggest challenges of self-diagnosing yourself as a star. It will require some digging, in the same way that learning about your status does. And in my conversations with potential stars, this is where most of them are off base. They have a skill, they know it's rare, but they overestimate how well they execute that skill relative to others. In stage two, I will help you get answers regarding where you rank relative to others—both at your current job and out there on the market.

How can I measure my own star status?

Start by going through the Three Things Exercise I introduced you to in the Crisis of Identity chapter.

Three Things Exercise

1. What is a task you do at work?

2. What is the skill required to execute that task?

3. What is the context in which the task is done?

In the Crisis of Identity chapter I used this exercise to help you develop a list of keeper skills when going through a major career transformation. We can use it here to evaluate whether any particular skill you have is related to your star status. Go through the exercise five times, with five skills, tasks, and contexts.

Next, for each skill you report, answer the following three questions:

1. Does this skill impact performance at work, either directly or indirectly?

   ☐ yes ☐ no

2. How many people at work have this skill?

   ☐ barely anyone   ☐ a lot of people
   ☐ a few people   ☐ most people
   ☐ some people

3. How good are you relative to others at work who also hold this skill?

☐ much worse
☐ a little worse
☐ about the same
☐ a little better
☐ much better

Next, let's go through each of the three-star criteria.

CRITERION ONE: THE SKILL IMPACTS MY PERFORMANCE AT WORK

I had a hundred people go through this exercise who "felt that they were underappreciated at work, and that their compensation or how they were treated doesn't match what they bring to the workplace." Just as I instructed you to do, they did the exercise five times, writing out five different skills. On average across the five skills, about 72 percent of them impacted performance at work, either directly or indirectly. Most people at this stage are eligible to be Underappreciated Stars. But as I will work through shortly, you need to satisfy all three criteria to be a true Underappreciated Star.

If you've answered yes to the performance question, next ask yourself, "*How* is each skill associated with performance?"

I asked this of the people in my study, and they were quite good at it, even when the link between the skill and performance wasn't obvious. For example, one person analyzes gene expression data (the task) using the skill of "bioinformatics expertise." They reported that "bioinformatics expertise directly impacts my performance at work by enabling me to effectively process and interpret complex genomic data, which is crucial for understanding the genetic basis of cancer and developing targeted therapies. Additionally, it indirectly contributes to the institution's success by facilitating data-driven decision making and advancing our research efforts in the fight against cancer." I love the scope of this answer; it not only captures the local influence of the skill on performance (developing targeted therapies), but also, the global one (advancing research efforts in the fight against cancer).

Let's consider another example, equally clear but simpler. A cashier at a store wrote that their skill of "speed and efficiency" impacts performance at work because when they're not efficient, "lines form, unhappy customers take away from other customers still shopping, leading to more unhappy customers not being helped, and the cycle continues." This person clearly articulated how a lack of efficiency leads to this iterative problem of angry people at the store.

As you think through your answers, what are the costs of executing your skill poorly? If you were to do a bad job, who would be impacted? Like the store clerk, your answer might be "everyone around me." Or the gene analyst, "all of cancer research." Understanding scope is also important as you think through your next job.

CRITERION TWO: THE SKILL IS RARE

How many of your skills are considered rare where you work? It can be tough to know how rare your skill is out in the world, but you probably have some sense of how you compare to others in your workplace. Across the five skills, about 11 percent of people reported that "barely anyone" held their skill; another 18 percent that a few people had it. These two groups—totaling 29 percent of the sample, are eligible to be Underappreciated Stars based on criteria two. Everyone else (some people, a lot of people, most people) made up the remaining 71 percent.

CRITERION THREE: I'M BETTER THAN OTHER PEOPLE AT THIS (RARE) SKILL

Now let's turn to the final criterion for being a star: you're better than other people at your skill. About 70 percent of the people in my study reported being either a little better (35 percent) or much better (another 35 percent) than other people at work. Given that most people experience the better-than-average effect, these data aren't surprising. There's definitely some self-serving biases going on (only 4 percent of people said they were "much worse" or "a little worse" than others).

LET'S BRING THESE THREE CRITERIA TOGETHER TO EVALUATE YOUR STAR STATUS

You don't need to satisfy all three criteria on every skill to qualify as a star, but you should satisfy all three for at least one skill. I evaluated the star status of each of the five skills people reported on. I gave a skill star status if it satisfied three things:

One, people reported that the skill is relevant to performance;

two, that "barely anyone" or "a few people" had the skill; and three, that they were either "a little better" or "much better" at the skill than others at work.

How many of your skills satisfy the Underappreciated Star criteria?

On average, 19 percent of the skills people reported on in my study qualify as star skills in that they check all three criteria boxes. But interestingly, about 48 percent of the people in the study qualify as an Underappreciated Star—they have at least one star skill that satisfied all three criteria. Most of us are probably Underappreciated Stars in a very limited capacity. We have about one star skill that sets us apart from the others.

At this stage you might be thinking, "Maybe I'm not as much of a star as I think I am?" If so, I urge you to continue reading. You still need to learn how your skills compare to others in your industry.

In what ways am I underappreciated at work?

Next, let's turn to the ways in which people feel underappreciated at work.

The most common forms of underappreciation fall into three categories. First is compensation; you aren't paid enough or given enough financial perks, given that you're a star. Second is opportunities. You're not on the right promotion trajectory or are not given the right training opportunities or chances to network at conferences or big company meetings.

Third is social status. The amount of respect and admiration you hold is too low given that you're a star. People don't listen to you when they should; you don't have enough influence over decisions, or you're not put on the important committees that help you climb up—roles that I labeled "visible" in the last two chapters.

I gave my hundred underappreciated people a list of fifteen dimensions that they felt underappreciated on (some of which you'll recognize from the Change List in the Runner-Up chapter). For each, they responded to this prompt: "Given my skills, I should be given more . . . ," with the option to check as many as they wanted. Here's that list. You can start by checking off all that apply.

APPRECIATION WISH LIST

1. Amount of responsibility

2. Leadership opportunities

3. Training opportunities

4. Promotion opportunities

5. Number of people I oversee

6. Leadership responsibilities

7. Flexibility in work hours

8. Say over how much I travel

9. Respect from coworkers

10. Respect from bosses

11. Work-life balance

12. Say over my schedule

13. Say over my working hours

14. Say over where I work

15. Influence over decisions

Next comes the hard part. Rank order your list of desires, from the most to least important. In the Drifted Apart chapter, I helped you develop a list of job preferences: must haves, things it would be nice to have, and things you're willing to cave on. Use these principles here. Be honest with yourself about your absolute deal-breakers and what you're willing to be flexible on. You probably won't get everything you want on this list, but prioritizing will help you in stage four, especially once you have a sense of your value on the market and you know what a company has to offer.

In my study, the top five most common dimensions are compensation (91 percent of people want more), promotion opportunities (65 percent), leadership opportunities (35 percent), respect from bosses (36 percent), and—tied for fifth place—respect from coworkers (31 percent) and influence over decisions (31 percent).

Aside from money, people want more status at work. They want to be respected (by bosses and coworkers), and they want to have influence.

Once you're comfortable with the label of Underappreciated Star and you have a sense of what you want, it's time to move on to stage one: why you're here.

Stage one: Why am I unhappy here?

In digging into the "why" piece in my interviews for this chapter, I realized that almost every person I spoke with had a different reason. One person felt like too much of her work was invisible to her boss because she worked from home; another felt frustrated that, despite how much her boss wanted to increase her salary, the company had a policy against it unless she had an offer from a competitor. The reasons are diverse, but they can be categorized into two dimensions: one, the degree to which your unique skill set is acknowledged by people at work; and two, the level at which the underappreciation occurs.

Let's start with the first dimension.

DOES MY WORKPLACE ACKNOWLEDGE MY SKILLS?

Think of how many people acknowledge that you have a unique set of skills at work. If you're anything like the participants in my study, the answer will be "not as much as they should." In my sample, about 54 percent of skills were acknowledged by coworkers and 55 percent by bosses. But about 26 percent of the time, no one acknowledges people's skills. That's a lot of skills going ignored.

As you go through this process, ask yourself two questions: Is my work done mostly behind the scenes, or is it visible to others? And if it is visible, who can see it? Other team members, or a person in power? Among the five skills people reported, about 62 percent are performed in front of coworkers, 52 percent in front of bosses. A good quarter of people's skills are performed in front of no one. There's a lot of solo work being done these days in the workplace (and working from home exacerbates this problem).

Most of us have a spotlight effect at work—we assume that the people around us are paying attention to our work, that our bosses register when we do a good job (even if they aren't around to witness it). Many don't, and you can help break your own bias by asking yourself these two questions: Who witnessed the work? Who acknowledged it?

There are a lot of reasons why skills go unseen and unacknowledged. In the Crisis of Identity chapter, I introduced you to Timothy, who, like the Underappreciated Star, has a skill set that sets him apart at work. He finds integrative solutions to problems that no one else finds. But nobody acknowledges his skill. Most people aren't around to witness his skill in action, and there's no system to document the quality of his work (his work uses a ticket system—either a request was answered, or it wasn't). His boss is constantly putting out fires so they rarely have time for feedback meetings. This deadly combination—work being unseen and not being acknowledged—makes him a prime example of how under-appreciation can happen.

You can take your Three Things Exercise and add these two questions for each skill:

4. Who acknowledges that you have this skill?

☐ coworkers   ☐ no one
☐ bosses   ☐ other

5. Who do you perform this skill in front of at work?

☐ coworkers   ☐ no one
☐ bosses   ☐ other

Having coworkers acknowledge your skill is important for having status at work in your teams. But having your boss or other leaders acknowledge it is important for promotions, compensation, and being appreciated in the ways that most stars care about. If you perform the skill in front of no one, you're facing an uphill battle when it comes to having that skill acknowledged. It's not a deal-breaker—plenty of independent contributors fall into this category—but there needs to be a system of keeping track of it. Timothy, for example, would often go above and beyond during his one-on-one meetings with people who submitted tickets (asking what else they needed help with that wasn't on the ticket). Customers valued this contribution, but there wasn't a mechanism to report it or even to give feedback on Timothy to his boss. His hard work was appreciated, but not by the right people.

AT WHAT LEVEL DOES THE UNDERAPPRECIATION OCCUR?

Next, think about the level at which underappreciation occurs. I use four categories, arranged from highest (encompassing the most people) to lowest: the market, your company, your role, and your interpersonal relationships at work. Let's go through each.

The market

At the highest level is the market. Imagine that no matter where you work, your skill set is not as valuable as you think it is, or as it used to be. Everyone with your skills is having trouble landing attractive jobs. A lot of people are feeling underappreciated at the market level these days. Take, for example, the advent of AI, which has led to a mass underappreciation of people at the market level. The CEO of IBM announced that 30 percent of back-office roles (those that don't involve human-to-human interfacing) would be replaced by AI. People won't be fired (yet) out of these roles, but attrition won't be mitigated with new hires. Other companies are following in their footsteps.

If there's been a shift in the market around how much your skills are prioritized and sought after, it's probably not just your company (or boss) that's behind you feeling underappreciated. About 44 percent of the people in my survey reported that "the market used to value my skills more than it does now," and 48 percent said that "people with skills like mine used to get paid a lot more than they do now in my industry."

A good percentage of people can feel their value slipping at the market level.

Your company

Next is the company where you work. The market might value your skill, but you work in a place where compensation, promotion, or other perks are determined by a set of rules that don't (only) have to do with your star status. Around 33 percent of people in my study agreed that "there are company-wide policies where I work around raises that apply to everyone, no matter what their role is." Subbu, whom I introduced you to in the Runner-Up chapter, experienced this problem. He needed a combination of things to be considered for a raise: a boss with power (which was also the case for 47 percent of people in my study) and a minimum amount of time at the company (64 percent of my sample). These policies applied to everyone, and Subbu, with his star status, was no exception.

As another example, some companies have a policy that raises are given only to people who have competitive offers from other companies (this is the case where I work, and the case for 24 percent of people in my study). You can be a star, but if no one is trying to scoop you, you'll make as much as the underperformers. And last, some companies don't have the resources to pay you, even if they wanted to (24 percent of people in my study). No one is getting a raise because the company can't afford it.

Your role

Next is the role that you hold. One of the more tragic reasons why people are Underappreciated Stars is because they hold precious roles at work—they are so good at their job that their boss is afraid to move them out of it. Zoe, the star salesperson I introduced you to in the Runner-Up chapter, held a precious role. She had a rich network of connections in her region and many return clients, which contributed to her stellar numbers. Her boss was reluctant to promote her out of this role not only because she didn't have "broad" connections across the United States, but also because she was one of the only salespeople to have clients who came back for more. Losing her repeat customers would mean a hit to their revenue. Around 22 percent of people in my study haven't been promoted because "there's no one to replace me in my current role" and 23 percent because "it's too expensive to replace me." About a quarter of the people I surveyed hold precious roles at work.

Your interpersonal relationships

And last, underappreciation can happen at the interpersonal level. Imagine that like Christine, you have a boss who relies on you to handle their communications with the team. You're the office glue, and without you the place would fall apart. Your boss realizes your utility—and they probably stop by your office ten times a day to get you to help them with something—and they have no intention of letting a good thing go. Or imagine that you have the opposite problem—a boss who acknowledges your skills, but sees you as competition. They're afraid you might pass them by one day, so they undercut you publicly or play down your performance to other leaders to keep you in your place.

Interpersonal reasons for not getting ahead were incredibly common in my sample. Around 39 percent of people think they haven't been promoted because they "hold their team together," 44 percent because they "carry the load of their team," 38 percent because their manager "relies on me to resolve conflicts within the team," and another 29 percent because they "manage conflicts between my boss and the team." And last, 32 percent because "my manager relies on me to do their work for them." A third of people in my study believe that they are doing their managers' jobs for them, which is why they're being held back.

In total, between a third and a half of people can pinpoint the specific interpersonal dynamics at work responsible for holding back their careers.

NOW THAT I HAVE SOME SENSE OF THE LEVEL AT WHICH UNDERAPPRECIATION OCCURS, WHAT DO I DO?

In my study, people could check as many reasons as they wanted for why they're underappreciated at work. The bad news is, they checked off a lot. You probably did as well. And they probably spanned all four levels. But the good news is, almost all the reasons why you're underappreciated now are detectable at the interview stage, if you ask the right questions. You can learn whether there are company-wide rules for promotions before you take a job. And you can network with current employees to learn about barriers at the role and interpersonal levels that will prevent you from being appreciated on the dimensions you care about. Asking the right questions during stages two and three can help you detect the likelihood that you will once again find yourself in underappreciation territory.

Stage two: What do I want my future career to look like?

In stage one, you've started to collect data on who acknowledges (or fails to acknowledge) your skills at work, and started to understand the level at which your underappreciation occurs. You've also ranked your list of appreciation dimensions that will guide your job search.

Understanding these things takes a lot of time and work; it won't happen overnight. If you don't have clear answers yet, don't worry. You can still move on to stage two—knowing what you want your future career to look like—before you have total clarity.

In stage two, I assume that you're highly identified with your career, and you plan on sticking with it. But if the stage one exercises led you to question this assumption, I urge you to read the first chapter on the Crisis of Identity career goer. You want to know where you want to go before you dive into stage two.

I've organized this stage around three big questions you need to ask yourself.

ARE YOU A STAR COMPARED TO THE PEOPLE YOU'RE COMPETING AGAINST?

I was chatting the other day with Jamie, an underappreciated star in law who, like many in her position, was fed up with the pay structure at her firm and was putting out feelers for a new job. "I'm covering the most cases, and I bill more hours than anyone else," she told me. "Plus, the clients prefer to meet with me over the other junior associates." Leading with these "better than those around me" stats, she figured finding a new job in a bigger firm (with a better pay structure) would be easy. But it wasn't.

Jamie, like many around her, fell victim to a common bias—she chose to make local comparisons to people on her team and her firm, and neglected to make global comparisons to people who are applying for her dream job from other companies. As I discussed in the Runner-Up chapter, your real competition is a pool of unknown talent. And for hirers, when it comes to comparing candidates to one another, context matters.

For Underappreciated Stars, all of whom have talent and skill, context usually means the company you work for—its reputation, how long it's been on the map, its size, and how hard it was to get a job there in the first place. These things can matter just as much (if not more) than your skills and accomplishments. Take two candidates with nearly identical accomplishments—Jamie at her small firm, and a fictitious competitor named Naia, who's also doing well at her big, well-established firm. There's a good chance that Naia will get the job, even if she isn't number one on her team. In fact, she might be in the top 20 percent at her company, and Jamie in the top 5 percent. For many organizations, the big fish in a small pond is often a less attractive option than even a medium-size fish in a medium-size pond.

Why?

There's a belief that prestigious companies (those that have been around for a long time, have a history of excellence, and are notoriously hard to break into) have higher-quality applicants coming out of them than less prestigious companies. People assume that the Naias of the world had to beat out stiffer competition to get their jobs than the Jamies of the world had to do to get their jobs. This is a stereotype, but there is a kernel of truth to it; firms with better reputations not only attract more applicants than firms with worse reputations, they also attract higher-quality candidates.

Because of this bias, it's important for the Underappreciated Star to figure out which companies other stars in the job pool are coming from. What are the reputations of those companies, and do those reputations matter more than performance, or other measures we think of as great equalizers? Your goal in stage two is to find out who your true relevant social comparisons are. Connect with someone who hires for a company you're interested in and ask: "For the last four hires, what organizations did people work at before they started here?" You will quickly gain reputation information about your potential future employers. Do they only hire from a handful of previous employers because they feel confident that the applicant will be high quality? Or perhaps it's not the prior employer who matters, it's where people were trained? Law school matters a lot for your first job at a firm, in the same way that whom you apprenticed with matters for becoming a chef or a hair stylist.

You can start by networking with those who hold your job but are better off than you on the dimensions that are on your checklist. Most well-established career goers have these network connections, but if you don't, check out the networking sections of the Crisis of Identity and Drifted Apart chapters for some tips that apply to you too.

YOU MIGHT BE GREAT AT YOUR SKILL, BUT FOR MOST COMPANIES IS "GOOD ENOUGH" JUST FINE?

During your networking conversations, probe into whether the places you want to work (or the industry more generally) care about greatness in the same way that you think they do.

There can be a diminishing returns problem with skills at work. At some point, you reach the good-enough stage, and organizations don't have a financial incentive for hiring truly excellent people. It costs them a lot to go from good to excellent, and most of the time the difference in quality doesn't affect their financial bottom line.

When I help newly minted PhDs get (nonacademic) industry jobs, I run into this problem a lot. My students are highly skilled statisticians; they're at the top of their game. But for most jobs (even those that require data analysis skills), you don't need much more than master's-level training. There are very few analytic engineer jobs that require more; those that do (which pay a lot) usually go to people trained in computer engineering, not psychology. I have to remind my students that their relevant social comparisons are usually master's-level applicants who can do rudimentary statistics, not PhDs in computer engineering, who can do a lot more. They often get tripped up on the commonality of having a PhD, but that's not the dimension that matters. The skill set is the dimension that matters. It's a cynical perspective, but it's rare to find an organization that treats the hiring of top talent like a sommelier treats rare vintages, appreciating the small differences among the best of the best. We do this when it comes to dating too. We might really want to date someone who is over six feet tall, but if 20 percent of the dating pool is full of six-footers and only 1 percent are over six feet, we compromise.

The best way to find out if "good enough" is what most companies go with is to follow the instructions I gave for the previous question: look at patterns in a company's last three or four hires. If you know someone who is hiring for your role, ask them, "Do you think that someone who is a level down from me [in my student's case, a master's-level candidate] is fine for this role? Is there a reason why someone with my pedigree or skill set would be hired instead?" Put the burden on your contacts to explain why a company would want to level up. What is the additional benefit they get by going for a star? To do this, you can start by going on company websites or LinkedIn pages and looking at the work histories of the last several hires. During the interview (in stage three), I encourage you to push the interviewer a bit on this issue. The best predictor of future behavior is past behavior, so if an organization plans to break the tradition of hiring "good enough" for you, they should be able to tell you why.

If you find that your whole industry has shifted to a good-enough model, then it's time to rethink your strategy of anchoring your search on your set of star skills. Think about how your combination of skills—not any of them on their own—sets you apart from the rest. Perhaps Jamie, my big-fish-in-a-small-pond lawyer, is really good at interfacing with a particular type of client, and that her skill lies in her ability to gain trust and work with fussy clients who are pains in the ass. Often, an unusual combination of skills is what lands the job. But only through networking can we learn how unusual our combination of skills is and what type of "unusual" a company goes for.

HOW MUCH TOLERANCE DO YOU HAVE FOR TAKING ON A JOB THAT MIGHT COME WITH MORE THAN YOU'VE BARGAINED FOR?

Most Underappreciated Stars are well versed in the world of risk-taking; they've done a lot of it throughout their careers to get this far. But by the time you get to the top, you might feel like you know exactly what you want out of job, and you aren't willing to take on one that has some critical unknown parts to it. Now you want to flex your skills, perform well, and get compensated for it.

I get it. As someone who hates uncertainty, I relate a lot to this mentality. But I've come to realize that everyone needs to take risks at work, even those of us who've acquired all the skills we think we need and want in order to spend the rest of our careers in familiar territory. I sat down with John Miles, a man of many careers, who attributes his repeated successes in life to a single thing: tolerance for risk-taking at all stages of his career.

John, a graduate of the United States Naval Academy, has succeeded at so many different things that talking to him made my
head spin. He has an illustrious background as a naval officer and
a seasoned senior executive at the C-level in Fortune 50 companies. He is the author of *Passion Struck*, hosts the number-one-
ranked alternative health podcast of the same name, and is an
enterprising systems entrepreneur. I'm naming just a few of the
things on his résumé.

It's no stretch to say that John has stature. But in talking with
him, it's clear that he never accepted the premise that his star status mattered much coming into a new job.

I asked John what he thinks holds the most talented people
back at work. He immediately turned to the fear of taking risks.
"One of the biggest things that happens is that people say no to
life-changing opportunities because of fear. I've tried to give people amazing opportunities. And more often than not, they say no
to them because they're outside their comfort zone," he told me.

When you're really good at what you do, learning something
new—and potentially failing at that thing—can feel much riskier
than it did when you were first starting out. You worry that your
failures will be in the spotlight; that a lot more people will potentially suffer because of the leadership roles you hold and
potentially fail at. You might feel that because you're a star you're
not supposed to have a steep learning curve at work. And you
might have gotten used to being incredible at everything you do,
which is certainly an addictive feeling. But taking on a little bit of
risk isn't a bad thing.

At this point, you want to collect data on the likelihood that a new job would come with some uncalculated risks and think deeply about your tolerance for that. For some, risk comes in the form of taking on a new leadership role you have no experience with. I interviewed for a job recently, and it was made clear that I would be in charge of mentoring all the assistant professors in the department (there were very few other people of my stature to do it, which is one of the reasons why they were interested in me). I felt okay with this risk level because despite not having done exactly what they wanted me to do before, I had enough experience in jobs adjacent to this one. But for some Underappreciated Stars, the jobs they're asked to do are totally outside of their comfort zone.

To assess potential risk, ask your network connections, "What surprising new things did you encounter on this job?" Frame your questions in the same way I framed the "Nobody told me that" exercise, not around "What risks did you encounter?" Not everyone sees surprises at work as risks—that's for you to determine.

Stage three: Go on a fact-finding mission to test whether a career is a good fit for you

Underappreciated Stars need to make sure that if they leave their current role, their calculated risks are likely to pay off. That they're not in for a repeat adventure, taking on a role full of potential that never materializes, leaving them underappreciated once again. During stage three I urge you to be open-minded but also cautious, to ask strategic questions around risk that help you predict what bumps in the road you'll encounter.

THE INTERVIEW PROCESS

Bring your "level of underappreciation" questions to your interviews

In stage one, you did a lot of work to understand the level at which your underappreciation occurs—from the market down to your interpersonal relationships with your coworkers and boss. In stage two, you figured out who your relevant social-comparison others are, to better understand which jobs you're likely to land. With these insights in your back pocket, you can now ask probing questions about potential levels of underappreciation during interviews.

I spoke with recruiter Vannessa Bogran, who's helped place people in all sorts of jobs—manufacturing, technology, sales, and marketing, to name a few. And when it comes to asking the eye-opening (but potentially awkward) question "How can I make sure I won't become underappreciated here should I take this job?" she recommends being as direct as possible.

I asked Vannessa how she manages situations in which she is trying to fill a role that she knows has problems—a boss who holds people back or a lack of support for the leaders, for example. These things are often red flags for the Underappreciated Star. She told me about a position she was recently trying to hire for that fit this bill. The boss was grinding people down (they had to ask permission to go to the bathroom), and they had massive turnover. No one stuck around for very long, especially the stars. Her calls with candidates were recorded, so she couldn't offer up information that was damning without being asked.

Vannessa told me that if you ask the pointed questions, you'll get honest answers (recruiters have reputations they care about, so they won't outright lie). For the Underappreciated Star, that means questions like: "Why are you hiring for this position, and what happened with the last few hires?" "Are there company-wide policies that dictate who is eligible for promotion opportunities?" "How many people from this boss's team have been promoted recently?"

To help get your list of questions started, here are several to ask during interviews, based on the reasons for underappreciation from stage one:

1. Are there company-wide policies around raises that apply to everyone, no matter what their job is?

2. Do people need to be working for a certain amount of time before they are eligible for a raise?

3. Do people need to get a competitive offer from elsewhere to get a raise?

4. How important is it that your boss has power in order for you to get a promotion or raise? *(Interviewers should be able to tell you what role your immediate supervisor plays in the promotion process.)*

5. Does the company typically have the budget to promote people regularly?

6. Is there a system in place to make sure that my role will be covered if I'm eligible for a promotion?

7. Have people not been promoted because they are too integral to their team?

8. Have people not been promoted because they play an integral role in managing conflicts either with their teams or between their boss and team?

DOES THIS JOB HAVE THE RIGHT KIND OF RISK FOR A STAR?

During this process, you also want to ask questions that help you decide whether you're taking the right kind of risk for someone who is already a star. There's often a bias toward believing that because you have star status on one dimension, you can easily achieve it on another, even if the two dimensions are only tangentially related. "Skills are teachable" is an adage I heard a lot from the people who hire. As an Underappreciated Star, you won't be convincing people that you can't learn new things. Your job will be to detect whether they have realistic expectations of how quickly you can do it, whether they will give you the support you need to get there, and whether the new skills you will need to learn overlap with the skills you already have (skills overlap is a topic I discussed a lot in the Stretched Too Thin chapter; you want to have fungibility among your skills).

Stars are often Hail Mary hires; the organization brings them in to save the day, but there's often nowhere to go but down. If the last three people failed at this role, or the role is ill defined and the organization uses language like "We're building the plane as we fly it," then you might be a Hail Mary hire. Subbu took on one of these roles once. He was promised a team to support him in a prestigious role—a carrot that was dangled in front of him for several months. But it never happened. He was a star without the structure in place to help him stay there.

One of the biggest reasons why incoming stars fail is because they aren't given the support structure they need—a well-paid team, financial resources, and support from the senior leaders. When you ask your questions, get concrete. How much of the budget is allocated to this role? How many people on my team have been hired and trained already? Or is the plan to hire me first, then build everything after, slowly over time?

Sometimes your smartest move is showing restraint. I wouldn't take a role that has no scaffolding in place to support it.

WILL YOU FACE A NEWCOMER HUMP WHEN YOU START A NEW JOB?

Many Underappreciated Stars are looking for more status at work. As I discussed above, three of the top five things the underappreciated want involve status (respect from bosses, respect from coworkers, and influence over decisions). And one of the main selling points of a fancy new job is just that. Come here, and you will get the respect you deserve and the decision-making power you deserve.

But as my research has found, bringing your status from one place to another is much more complicated than we think. When starting a new job, you might face a newcomer hump that you didn't anticipate—people don't care that you were fancy at your old job; you have to earn it from scratch at your new one. And one of the difficulties you might face is getting people to listen to you, even on dimensions in which you have expertise.

To illustrate this basic problem, my colleague Oana Dumitru and I ran a series of studies testing how much influence newcomers have in shaping group decisions. Some of these newcomers had status coming into the group, and some didn't. And at the end of the day, people didn't really listen to them, no matter how much status they had.

We had people who were strangers meet each other in pairs, spend about ten minutes working through a decision-making task, and then had a third person join them for a new task— figuring out who to hire among four job candidates. Across 370 groups, newcomers didn't influence decision-making as much as the two people in the original pair did, regardless of their status coming into the group. Speaking up as a newcomer was quickly shot down, even if they made important points. By the end of the study, newcomers, regardless of their status or their contributions to the group, were seen as less competent than the original two members by the people on their own team. It didn't matter what they did; the incompetence label stuck with them.

In organizations, the newcomer is up against a lot more: there are norms they don't know about and they might encounter new jargon. All the things I introduced you to in the Crisis of Identity chapter can make it tough for you to break into a new field or team.

The best way for you to gauge what your newcomer hump will be is to talk to other newcomers who, like you, came in with status. Once you're far along in the interview process, ask to be connected with them. They don't need to have your role or work in the same function as you, but they do need to be high-status outsiders when they came in. What hidden barriers did they face in influencing decisions that no one told them about? Were there stereotypes about outsiders coming in with status that they had to contend with? Only organizational insiders can help you figure out what your newcomer hump might look like.

HOW CAN YOU MAKE SURE YOU WILL BE A STAR IN YOUR NEW ORGANIZATION?

One of the biggest issues newcomers run into is the process of knowledge transfer—and this especially applies to newcomers who are stars. They have a lot of tacit knowledge and skills, but most of their experience applying these skills is in one workplace—their past one. How difficult (or easy) will it be to bring your knowledge and expertise from your old job to your new one? If you interview for a company that, despite having hired a lot in the last few years, still does things the same old way, they probably have a knowledge-transfer problem. It's not that they can't bring in fresh talent, it's that there's no process in place for that talent to transfer their knowledge to their teams. You need a good knowledge-transfer plan in place to hold on to your star status in your new organization.

There's a lot of research on knowledge transfer in organizational psychology. Most of this work focuses on how people transfer knowledge across generations within a company. For example, millennials are "digital natives"—they are constantly connected to social media, and a lot of their knowledge transfer happens online. Boomers, on the other hand, like to transfer knowledge via three-hour lunches or informal water-cooler conversations. Tell them to check the local Slack channel and they will roll their eyes at you.

One factor that is a huge predictor of knowledge transfer across all types of organizations is an organization's *absorptive capacity*. In short, absorptive capacity is the ability of an organization to recognize the value of new information (like all the expertise you bring as a star newcomer), assimilate it, and exploit it for their benefit. It's an abstract concept, but here's a concrete example.

Imagine that you're a biologist who studies slime molds. As a newcomer, you bring your latest discovery with you. But you didn't just discover a new slime, you discovered a new way of discovering slime. You invented a new slime-detection tool. Imagine that you share your new discovery in a big company meeting. Following that meeting, does the company share your discovery with other parts of the organization? Do they use your new slime-detection tool to change how they now study slime molds, including where they go to look for new types of them? Or do they say, "Thanks for the cool presentation," then go back to their old, well-established way of finding slime?

Many Underappreciated Stars are shocked that their metaphorical slime-mold discoveries die with the meeting. That despite how much utility they bring to the organization, their knowledge and expertise never gets utilized or recognized. Getting the organization or even their team to take them seriously—and to make real changes—is a fruitless endeavor. Many of us know what this absorptive capacity experience feels like in our own personal relationships. Every time I visit my mother, I try to get her to order her groceries online to make her life easier. But she won't do it. She would rather drive an hour to get lettuce. If she was a company and I was a newly hired Underappreciated Star, I would be banging my head against the wall.

Knowledge transfer is a social process, and the organization you're interviewing for should have an explicit plan for how to execute it. Ask questions like "What is the plan to make sure my knowledge of X, or my expertise of Y, gets taught here?" and "Will I be invited to strategic planning meetings to help figure out the best way to do this?" (And then offer to run those meetings.) At my workplace, knowledge transfer takes the form of workshops where people teach their latest discoveries. We have an explicit goal to transfer knowledge, and you can see that by looking at how many cross-team meetings we hold where people from different areas come together to learn new things.

Stage four: Landing the job you will love

Underappreciated Stars often don't go through the same application process as other career goers, especially those who are advanced in their careers. They are recruited, asked to apply for a job, or given information about the availability of a position before it's publicly posted. Every single job I've been offered in the last five years I was first asked to apply for.

That said, once I got the interview, I wasn't a shoo-in. There were other experts also interviewing, many of whom had advantages over me. In my interviews with recruiters and hiring managers, I've learned that the single biggest mistake that advanced people make is assuming that the interview is purely one-way at this stage: it's the star who is doing the interviewing, the star isn't being interviewed. Treat this interview like a first date. Yes, you're an expert, but you both want to make sure the fit is there.

THINK ABOUT HOW YOU WANT TO BE COMPENSATED BEYOND SALARY

About half of the underappreciated in my study think that it would be hard to find a job that would pay as much as they want. Yet over 90 percent of these same people want to be paid more. At some point, you will probably need to get creative with what other dimensions of appreciation you're willing to consider. Coming into an interview with a financial bottom line that isn't realistic won't land you the job. Bring your ranked list of appreciation dimensions with you to interviews. And think creatively; companies love to see candidates ask for compensation in ways that also signal commitment. For example, propose a compensation structure that builds in promotion and training opportunities on a clearly defined timeline. Build in concrete steps that the organization will take to ensure that you have support for your role.

Consider asking for things like "at least three full-time experts on my team who are trained and hired by the time I start, along with three paid workshops a year for these experts to attend to hone their skills in X." And when it comes time for compensation requests, remember that money is fungible. The organization might not be willing to give you a higher base salary, but they will be willing to comp you indirectly with perks. I met someone who negotiated for a year of full-time child care, another for several months of a cleaning service. The organization had big contracts with places like cleaning companies, so it cost them less to get someone a yearly cleaning subscription than it would have cost this person to book it themself.

What you don't want to agree to is putting your pay on layaway; for example, agreeing to terms like having your salary go up once the organization gets $1 million more in financial backing from an angel investor. Getting paid tomorrow for the work you're doing today is not a form of compensation. But giving you a big bonus if you're still in the company after three years is.

LEARN HOW TO TALK ABOUT YOUR SKILLS IN A GENERAL WAY SO THE COMPANY CAN MAKE COMPARISONS

In this chapter and the Crisis of Identity chapter, I had you go through the Three Things Exercise to help you learn how to talk about your skills in a way that is closely tied to outcomes. Underappreciated Stars often get too local with those outcomes, which can make it hard for an organization to see how their performance at their last job will translate to performance in this one.

When explaining to people what your skills are (or putting them on your résumé), talk about outcomes using a bottom line that everyone understands. This is especially the case if you work for a small company and you're looking to move up to a bigger one. For example, if you say, "I helped increase revenue by 30 percent," say 30 percent of what ("from $100,000 in revenue to $130,000 in revenue"). The clearer you can be about what company-wide outcomes you would contribute to, the better.

When we fail to do this, there's often an assumption that the outcome is not that impressive. Companies prefer certainty in knowing what a performance metric means at a specific company. If this metric isn't widely known—meaning you don't work for a Fortune 500 company that sets the industry standard for these things—they will default to assuming that you're not as big of a star as you might be.

I see this happen a lot when people are applying to graduate school. Without standardized measures like GRE or MCAT tests—which everyone used to have to take but no longer does—there's a bias toward admitting people who come from the most prestigious institutions because the admissions committee feels like it knows what a candidate's score "ought to have been" should they have taken it. If you got straight As as a physics major at Harvard, your math score on a standardized test would probably be high. What about straight As at a lesser-known school? In the minds of the admissions committee, who knows what that test score would have been. Spelling out your accomplishments in ways that allow people to make direct comparisons will reduce the likelihood that you'll run into this bias.

LEARN WHAT THE ACHILLES' HEEL OF THE COMPANY IS, AND USE IT TO YOUR ADVANTAGE

John Miles would go to great lengths to convince a company that they had an Achilles' heel, and that he was the perfect person to help repair it.

"I once did a consulting job at JPMorgan Chase. I was tasked with a seemingly insurmountable challenge: to test the security of what they claimed was an impenetrable data center. It was a bold claim, and with a team of former special operators at my side, we were determined to put it to the test. We scouted the premises, identifying a subtle vulnerability—the access points for their generator gas tanks. It was a pathway overlooked by many, but not by us," John told me.

"In a carefully orchestrated maneuver, we used these gas tank access points as our entry. Climbing through this unguarded gateway, we navigated our way stealthily, moving with precision and purpose. Finally, after navigating through the layers of defense, we found ourselves right where they thought we couldn't be— inside the data center, standing on the very floor they believed was untouchable."

You don't need to have John's stealth skills to figure out what an organization's pain points are. But doing a little digging ahead of time, and thinking through how you can address those needs, can get you pretty far. At one job I interviewed for, I learned ahead of time that the junior faculty were struggling with grant writing and had very few senior professors who had written successful grants to mentor them. One brief conversation with a network connection taught me this. During my interview, I showed them my mentorship plan for grant writing. It showed a level of sensitivity to the needs of the workplace that most senior people didn't show.

In some cases, what an organization needs isn't just your star skill set, it's a combination of skills that are rarely seen together. Perhaps there are a lot of people who have excellent technical skills like you, but they don't also have good mentorship skills. Your combination of skills, even if any one of those skills doesn't make you a star, really increases your chances of landing the job.

■ ■

TAKE-HOMES FOR EACH STAGE

STAGE ONE:

- Before you assume you're a star, evaluate the label by asking yourself three questions: Do you have a skill that is relevant to the workplace? Is that skill rare? Are you better at this skill than others?

- Measure your own star status by analyzing whether your main skills fit the criteria, which I teach you to do borrowing from the Three Things Exercise from the Crisis of Identity chapter.

- To understand why you're unhappy, focus on two questions: Does my workplace acknowledge my skills? What is the level at which the underappreciation occurs? (It could include the market, your company, your role, and/or your interpersonal relationships.)

STAGE TWO:

- Work out who you are competing against.

- Figure out whether the organization wants stars or is fine with average performers.

- Identify how much risk you're willing to take to move to a new position that is different from one you're in now, and assess the risk of the new position if they are promising you the world.

STAGE THREE:

- Bring your level-appreciation questions from stage two to the interview.

- Learn whether a new job would involve more uncertainty than you're comfortable taking on at this stage of your career.

STAGE FOUR:

- Think creatively about how you want to be compensated, and that includes moving beyond your salary.

- Learn how to talk about your skills in general terms so that the company can make appropriate comparisons to your competitors.

- Learn what the Achilles' heel of a company is so you can use it to your advantage. Many companies need stars like you, but they don't know it. You can leverage your unique combination of skills to convince them why they do.

■ ■

Final Thoughts

...

G etting to the bottom of why you're unhappy at work is complicated business. Just as complicated, I would argue, as understanding why you've drifted apart from your spouse ten years into marriage, or why you've struggled to have a stable, trusting relationship with your adult child. All relationships—including the one you have with your career—can go wrong in a multitude of ways. As a relationships scientist, I've understood for a long time that the only way to repair fractured, damaged relationships is to take a step back and spend some time carefully evaluating how you got here. To get out of the forward-thinking mindset just for a moment and spend some time processing your psychological state of mind. Relationships rarely fall apart because of the actions of just one person—we all contribute, in one way or another, even if we have a hard time seeing how. In this book, I've asked you to think carefully about how everyone involved—from your entire profession, to the organization where you work, to you—has played a part.

Throughout the process of writing this book, it was never lost on me that I'm asking a lot of the reader. I've asked you to rethink your whole career strategy, from whom you should network with, to what should be in your job materials, to what questions you should ask during interviews. And besides these concrete steps, there's the work of digging deep to understand your psychological starting place. People spend years in therapy on the metaphorical stage one of each chapter, unpacking the question "Why am I unhappy here?"

For many, answering this question means taking two steps forward and one step back. You might find, for example, that halfway through stage two you learn from chatting with people that you've changed in ways you didn't realize. In fact, I suspect that the process of forming new social connections will teach you things about yourself that you wouldn't have discovered by using my self-assessment tools alone. We often rely on our social relationships to help us process changes in our lives, including our relationships. It's why we spend hours talking about new relationships and breakups with our close others. The same is true of our relationships with our careers. And as with any change, be patient with yourself if the journey is windier than you'd hoped. When it comes to career discovery, slow and steady wins the race.

Before you depart, there are a few additional lessons I want to leave you with. Most of these are lessons that I learned during my interviews with people who have made career changes. One of the reasons why I dedicate so much of this book to the art of networking is because of how much I learned from doing so. The wisdom of someone who's been through a career change (or helped someone else go through one) and is willing to get candid about it is worth its weight in gold.

Lean in to your emotions. They're invaluable in helping you process a career change.

In the chapter on the Drifted Apart, I introduced you to Tricia Baker, the school psychologist turned therapist who realized that a career in school psychology was no longer for her. She spent hours doing paperwork and managing relationships between the people handling a case, not helping at-risk youth, which is what she always wanted to do. Tricia went back to school, got a (new) master's, and is now happily working as a therapist doing tele-health. What I didn't tell you about Tricia is that her career transition was unusual for one specific reason: she had known for years that she wanted to be a therapist, long before she became a school psychologist. But for practical reasons, she went into school psychology instead. It was a classic case of following your head instead of your heart.

The breaking point for Tricia was the few agonizing months she spent sitting (literally) across the room from the people who had her dream job. School psychologists have routine meetings with all the people involved in overseeing a case, including administrators, lawyers, and the therapists who work directly with their clients. For Tricia, sitting with these therapists was like sitting across the table from your unrequited love and their new partner, listening to them carry on about how happy they are, arms wrapped around each other. There were days she felt like crying right there in the middle of the meeting.

The emotions Tricia felt during these final two months ran deep. She was envious of these people and their jobs. She was angry at herself for making a career choice in her early twenties that she now felt stuck with, and she was resentful of the circumstances that led to her decision. "I found myself in a very political job, far removed from the helping process," she told me. Politics aren't for Tricia, and she added "uncomfortable in my own skin" to the long list of feelings she was contending with. Tricia didn't face the uncertainty that most career transitioners face. She wasn't overwhelmed with the prospect of starting over because she didn't know what it would take to get there; she knew exactly what it took. And she wasn't worried about forming a new social network from scratch; she had these network connections. Because of the time spent around therapists, coupled with her background in psychology from college, she knew the norms and the jargon and the hidden curriculum.

As someone on the outside who was looking in, it seemed obvious to me what the smart choice was. But competing against all these things that were screaming at her to "get out now!" was a strong emotion that most of us are familiar with: guilt.

When I asked Tricia to elaborate on the barriers she faced to leaving school psychology, she didn't lead with practical issues, and there were plenty. She led with how she felt. "There was so much guilt. I had a family at the time. I was deciding whether to cut income for my family, take time away from kids to go back to school," she told me. And when she sat down with her partner to decide what to do, they spent almost the entire conversation talking about her feelings. Yes, there were big things to consider, like how to pay for another master's degree. But first they needed to unpack her emotional state of mind. They worked through what the experience of chronic envy and regret was doing to her mental health, and whether it was a good thing to let her feelings of guilt win.

It helps that as someone who works in the mental health space, Tricia is a master at labeling emotions, working through them, and teaching the same skill to others. She also knows that leading with practicalities can shape the decision-making process in ways we often don't foresee. The reasons why she had chosen school psychology were practical ones, and so, too, would be the reasons for staying. If she was to stay in the field, she needed to be able to say to herself, "I've decided to stay in this career for financial reasons. But I'm doing this knowing that I'm signing up for a lifetime of envy and regret." If she wasn't comfortable making that statement, she told herself, she wasn't ready to give up on her dream to change careers.

Once Tricia started the transition—quitting her old job and going back to school—she faced a new wave of emotions. "We couldn't afford the online [master's] program, so I was commuting two hours each way a day," she said. The guilt lingered, and feelings of envy were replaced with feelings of ambivalence. It wasn't as if things went from dark and depressing to bright and delightful overnight. Those hours sitting in rush-hour traffic, knowing she was going to get home after her kids were in bed, were tough. But again, she labeled her feelings and worked through them. "If I felt ambivalent about my choice, I talked about it," she said. "And now that I'm on the other side of things, I try to be totally open with people about what the emotional ups and downs will be." For Tricia, who works with at-risk teens, clear, honest communication about your feelings, and honesty with yourself and others about those feelings, is an essential part of development. "No one moves on, really, from any relationship without going through this critical step," she told me.

I noticed a trend among my successful career transitioners that matches Tricia's experience. They all used emotion-based language when discussing their journeys. Instead of saying things like "First I explored what new certifications I would need to get, and then I looked up the pay scale for different careers," they said things like "I first had to get to the source of my low self-esteem. Why was the work that used to bring me joy now making me feel bad about myself?" Susan, the professor turned UX researcher I introduced you to in the Crisis of Identity chapter, is a prime example of this.

The moment you start thinking about a job or career transition, label your emotions. Bring them front and center, and don't dismiss them as trite or irrelevant. Sometimes we don't think that logical decisions are emotion-based ones, but we are kidding ourselves. Social scientists have been studying the role of emotions in guiding decision-making for many years; emotions will exert their influence, but how and when can be up to you. The best advice I can give you is to follow what Tricia did: label them, talk about them, and fold them into the language you use around your decisions. You'll likely experience different emotions in each of the four stages, and you'll have some days that are more emotional than others. This is all part of the process; it's not a red flag that something is wrong.

It's okay to have mixed feelings about leaving a job. You don't need to be ready to leave before you start exploring.

One of the biggest misconceptions people have about leaving a job or career, or frankly leaving any relationship, is that one day you will wake up and feel ready. That a magical light will switch on, telling you that the uncertainty stage is over and it's time to move on to the next thing. You might also think that as you become more experienced and seasoned at work, your feelings of uncertainty and ambivalence about your choices will go away. Successful people and those in power often come across as more confident than their less-experienced counterparts.

But as I learned, it's not that successful people don't experience mixed feelings, especially around their careers; it's that they've learned to live with them. They label the emotion like Tricia did, and then embrace it as part of the process. In fact, "embracing uncertainty" was a theme that came up during almost all my conversations with seasoned career transitioners. John Miles, who's made a lot of dramatic career moves, is a prime example of this. In the chapter on the Underappreciated Star, John talked about how the fear of uncertainty is the biggest thing holding people back. Often when we're junior or less experienced, we read a lot into our internal "uncertainty" signals; we think that if we aren't

100 percent sure of our decision, we aren't ready to take a leap. Decision paralysis kicks in, and we wait for that magical day when we feel "ready" to come before we make a move. From John's perspective, we shouldn't read too much into these feelings, and we certainly shouldn't wait for that magical day. In fact, using uncertainty as a compass can prevent you from taking necessary risks.

I designed this book to allow you to move at any pace you're comfortable with, especially early on, when you're still employed at the job you're thinking of leaving. But sometimes, even the simple thought of exploring an alternative career is so threatening to people that they shy away from moving from stage one to stage two. If you have mixed feelings during this stage transition, that's okay. Like John Miles taught me, don't read too much into it. Certainty shouldn't be thought of as a prerequisite to starting the career transition process. It should be thought of as something that increases as you move through it.

Frank conversations are an essential part of your career journey, even if they feel uncomfortable at times.

Throughout this book, I gave you a lot of advice on how to talk to people—from new acquaintances who work in careers you're exploring, to recruiters and hiring managers, to interviewers. The questions I urge you to ask are specific, get at the heart of what a career or job is like, and, above all else, are blunt. In stages three and four (which focus on the interview process) you might at times feel like I've asked you to trade in your desire to be liked for your desire to uncover the truth. I have indeed asked you to flip the power dynamics around, treating the interviewer as an information provider, not just an evaluator.

If frankness isn't your style, I understand if this advice feels like a tall order. The norm to engage in polite, indirect communication can influence all of us, especially if we're trying to fit in or make a good impression. But unlike other norms at work, this norm is often born out of pluralistic ignorance. People assume that if everyone else is avoiding real talk, it's because they don't like it. But in reality most people actually prefer keeping it real; they're just afraid to violate the norm.

Tricia, who is quick to embrace politeness norms, understands this concern. "I shy away from being super direct," she told me. It took a few times of working through the "very specific question approach" to get her on board. But what converted her was how pleasantly surprised interviewers were to get these types of questions. "It was like a breath of fresh air, being asked specific questions about the job, and they didn't feel like they were being interrogated at all," she said. No one likes to have their time wasted, and by asking these questions, it was clear to the interviewers that Tricia valued their time as much as she valued her own.

In this book I've carefully vetted all the "real talk" questions I suggest you ask during stages three and four, being mindful of the power dynamics at play. The goal isn't to come across as abrasive, but to showcase that you're truly interested in finding out about fit, which is a goal the person on the other end of the conversation also has. Throughout your conversations, I urge you to engage in what psychotherapist and relationships expert Esther Perel calls "investigative questions"—questions that are specific and get to the heart of what you need to know. Esther talks about how asking these types of questions can help couples move past an affair, but the logic applies as well to moving on from a failed work relationship. If you feel nervous about being frank, remember this: everyone involved wants compatibility, and the only way to find out if you have it is to be open and honest from the get-go.

ACKNOWLEDGMENTS

First and foremost, thanks to my editor, Lydia Yadi, who saw potential in this book at the stage when it was just a morsel of an idea. I will be forever grateful to Lydia for her constant attention to detail and her willingness to push me to perspective-take, thinking about what the experience of this book is like for the reader. From the title down to what studies made the cut, this book wouldn't have landed in its current form without Lydia. She's a gem of an editor. I would like to thank Megan McCormack, my other editor, whose thoughtful, clear comments kept me tethered to the idea that I need to capture people's emotional experiences at work. Megan reminded me throughout the writing process that a relationship with a job or career is like any other type of relationship, and she provided help in pointing out places in the book where I needed to remind the reader of this.

Writing a book that includes lots of new data takes a team, and my team included one invaluable member: Quincey Pyatt. Quincey not only helped program and execute the studies in this book, but she did so on tight time frames, anticipating my needs long before I did. I often felt like Quincey had an invisible hand propping me up through the research process, making sure I didn't fall flat on my back.

My graduate students (past and present) are the source of creativity in my life as a researcher, and much of their work found its way into this book. Thank you to Oana Dumitru, whose dissertation work on status and the experience of being a newcomer in teams was critical for the chapter on the Underappreciated Star. Thank you to Kareena del Rosario, whose work on physiology and stress, and the impact of stress on our day-to-day lives and on how we work alongside others, influenced much of my thinking for this book.

There are numerous people I interviewed for this book who provided insights, from recruiters and hiring managers who willingly shared their tricks of the trade, to career transitioners and job seekers who were willing to share their experiences with me, to academics who shared unique insights. Time is an important resource, and I will be forever grateful to these people for giving me some of theirs.

Thank you to my family, who were patient with me as I wrote in weird places and at weird times, and on more than one family vacation.

And last but certainly not least, thank you to my agent, Nathaniel Jacks, who entertains my half-baked ideas, helps me carve them into something real, and is a relentless supporter of my work. I would not be where I am as an author without Nat.

NOTES

OPENING

xiv **risk factors of divorce:** Paul R. Amato, "Research on Divorce: Continuing Trends and New Developments," *Journal of Marriage and Family* 72, no. 3 (June 18, 2010): 650–66, https://doi.org/10.1111/j.1741-3737.2010.00723.x.

xxviii **this stress test:** Amie M. Gordon and Wendy Berry Mendes, "A Large-Scale Study of Stress, Emotions, and Blood Pressure in Daily Life Using a Digital Platform," *Proceedings of the National Academy of Sciences* 118, no. 31 (July 29, 2021), https://doi.org/10.1073/pnas.2105573118.

CHAPTER 1: THE CRISIS OF IDENTITY

7 **two components of identity:** Colin Wayne Leach et al., "Group-Level Self-Definition and Self-Investment: A Hierarchical (Multi-component) Model of In-Group Identification," *Journal of Personality and Social Psychology* 95, no. 1 (July 2008): 144–65, https://doi.org/10.1037/0022-3514.95.1.144.

19 **observed 136 career goers:** Shoshana R. Dobrow and Monica C. Higgins, "Developmental Networks and Professional Identity: A Longitudinal Study," *Career Development International* 10, no. 6/7 (2005): 567–83, https://doi.org/10.1108/13620430510620629.

25 **people are much more willing:** Gillian M. Sandstrom, Erica J.

Boothby, and Gus Cooney, "Talking to Strangers: A Week-Long Intervention Reduces Psychological Barriers to Social Connection," *Journal of Experimental Social Psychology* 102 (September 2022): 104356, https://doi.org/10.1016/j.jesp.2022.104356.

29 **NPR ran a social experiment:** Linton Weeks, "I Was Absent That Day," NPR, July 4, 2011, www.npr.org/2011/07/05/137443123/i-was-absent-that-day.

32 **concepts used by insiders:** Ronald S. Burt and Ray E. Reagans, "Team Talk: Learning, Jargon, and Structure versus the Pulse of the Network," *Social Networks* 70 (July 2022): 375–92, https://doi.org/10.1016/j.socnet.2022.05.002; Lars Thøger Christensen, Dan Kärreman, and Andreas Rasche, "Bullshit and Organization Studies," *Organization Studies* 40, no. 10 (January 2019): 1587–1600, https://doi.org/10.1177/0170840618820072.

32 **piece on killing jargon:** Alison Roller, "No More New Normal: Buzzwords Employees Can't Stand," HRMorning, March 6, 2023, www.hrmorning.com/news/annoying-buzzwords.

32 **insiderspeak allows them:** Burt and Reagans, "Team Talk," 375–92.

33 **jargon at work can signal:** Alessandro Duranti, *A Companion to Linguistic Anthropology* (Malden, MA: Blackwell Publishing, 2005).

33 **common form of jargon:** Zachariah C. Brown, Eric M. Anicich, and Adam D. Galinsky, "Compensatory Conspicuous Communication: Low Status Increases Jargon Use," *Organizational Behavior and Human Decision Processes* 161 (November 2020): 274–90, https://doi.org/10.1016/j.obhdp.2020.07.001.

40 **the more senior people become:** Brown, Anicich, and Galinsky, "Compensatory Conspicuous Communication," 274–90.

CHAPTER 2: THE DRIFTED APART

67 **changes to core personality traits:** Nathan W. Hudson, Jaime Derringer, and Daniel A. Briley, "Do People Know How They've Changed? A Longitudinal Investigation of Volitional Personality Change and Participants' Retrospective Perceptions Thereof," *Journal of Research in Personality* 83 (December 2019): 103879, https://doi.org/10.1016/j.jrp.2019.103879.

68 **want to improve over time:** Nathan W. Hudson and R. Chris Fraley, "Do People's Desires to Change Their Personality Traits Vary with

Age? An Examination of Trait Change Goals Across Adulthood," *Social Psychological and Personality Science* 7, no. 8 (July 20, 2016): 847–56, https://doi.org/10.1177/1948550616657598.

72 **U.S. Bureau of Labor Statistics:** "Employment Projections," U.S. Bureau of Labor Statistics, www.bls.gov/emp/#:~:text=Total%20employ ment%20is%20projected%20to,in%20healthcare%20and%20social %20assistance.

72 **McKinsey & Company provides a breakdown:** James Manyika et al., "Jobs Lost, Jobs Gained: What the Future of Work Will Mean for Jobs, Skills, and Wages," McKinsey & Company, November 28, 2017, www.mckinsey.com/featured-insights/future-of-work/jobs-lost -jobs-gained-what-the-future-of-work-will-mean-for-jobs-skills -and-wages.

CHAPTER 3: THE STRETCHED TOO THIN

94 **According to the World Economic Forum:** Anatoli Colicev and Tuuli Hakkarainen, "5 Is the Perfect Number of Projects to Juggle. Here's Why," World Economic Forum, October 14, 2022, www.weforum .org/agenda/2022/10/work-projects-productivity-workload-burnout.

97 **don't know the hidden curriculum:** Rita Zeidner, "Beware of Mission Creep," SHRM, March 14, 2022, www.shrm.org/hr-today/news /hr-magazine/spring2022/pages/get-a-grip-on-mission-creep.aspx.

97 **promise of visibility:** Shahidul Hassan, "The Importance of Role Clarification in Workgroups: Effects on Perceived Role Clarity, Work Satisfaction, and Turnover Rates," *Public Administration Review* 73, no. 5 (July 23, 2013): 716–25, https://doi.org/10.1111/puar.12100.

100 **those with a flat hierarchy:** Gloria Mark, Victor M. Gonzalez, and Justin Harris, "No Task Left Behind?," *Proceedings of the SIGCHI Conference on Human Factors in Computing Systems* (April 2, 2005): 321–30, https://doi.org/10.1145/1054972.1055017.

101 **The average worker experiences:** Judy Wajcman and Emily Rose, "Constant Connectivity: Rethinking Interruptions at Work," *Organization Studies* 32, no. 7 (July 13, 2011): 941–61, https://doi.org/10.1177 /0170840611410829.

101 **we spend about two hours:** Jonathan B. Spira and Joshua B. Feintuch, "The Cost of Not Paying Attention: How Interruptions Impact Knowledge Worker Productivity," September 2005, http://iorgforum.org/wp

-content/uploads/2011/06/CostOfNotPayingAttention.BasexReport
.pdf.

105 **our ability to form memories of these tasks:** Victor M. Gonzalez
and Gloria Mark, "'Constant, Constant, Multi-Tasking Craziness':
Managing Multiple Working Spheres," *Proceedings of the SIGCHI
Conference on Human Factors in Computing Systems* (April 2004):
113–20, https://doi.org/10.1145/985692.985707.

110 **juggled multiple roles:** Mark, Gonzalez, and Harris, "No Task Left
Behind?," 21–30.

118 **found that information workers:** Gonzalez and Mark, "'Constant,
Constant, Multi-Tasking Craziness,'" 113–20.

121 **special collections viewing:** Michael Koncewicz, "Interacting with
the Edible Book: Ben Denzer's 20 Slices of American Cheese," The
Back Table, April 13, 2021, https://wp.nyu.edu/specialcollections/2021
/04/13/interacting-with-the-edible-book-ben-denzers-20-slices
-of-american-cheese.

CHAPTER 4: THE RUNNER-UP

143 **people on average are pretty:** Cameron Anderson et al., "Knowing
Your Place: Self-Perceptions of Status in Face-to-Face Groups," *Journal of Personality and Social Psychology* 91, no. 6 (December 2006):
1094–110, https://doi.org/10.1037/0022-3514.91.6.1094.

148 **how much status other people have:** Siyu Yu and Gavin J. Kilduff,
"Knowing Where Others Stand: Accuracy and Performance Effects
of Individuals' Perceived Status Hierarchies," *Journal of Personality
and Social Psychology* 119, no. 1 (July 2020): 159–84, https://doi.org
/10.1037/pspi0000216.

151 **how jolts influence:** Elijah X. Wee, Rellie Derfler-Rozin, and Jennifer
Carson Marr, "Jolted: How Task-Based Jolts Disrupt Status Conferral
by Impacting Higher and Lower Status Individuals' Generosity," *Journal of Applied Psychology* 108, no. 5 (May 2023): 750–72, https://doi
.org/10.1037/apl0001047.

164 **creators of jobs:** Jack Kelly, "There's Another Type of Inflation to Be
Concerned About: Corporate-Title Inflation," *Forbes*, July 14, 2022,
www.forbes.com/sites/jackkelly/2022/07/10/theres-another-type
-of-inflation-to-be-concerned-about-corporate-title-inflation/?sh
=3c65da7a5ee2.

CHAPTER 5: THE UNDERAPPRECIATED STAR

192 **CEO of IBM announced:** Katherine Tangalakis-Lippert, "IBM Halts Hiring for 7,800 Jobs That Could Be Replaced by AI, Bloomberg Reports," *Business Insider*, May 1, 2023, www.businessinsider.com/ibm -halts-hiring-for-7800-jobs-that-could-be-replaced-by-ai-report -2023-5.

192 **Other companies are following:** Aaron Mok and Jacob Zinkula, "ChatGPT May Be Coming for Our Jobs. Here Are the 10 Roles That AI Is Most Likely to Replace," *Business Insider*, September 4, 2023, www.businessinsider.com/chatgpt-jobs-at-risk-replacement -artificial-intelligence-ai-labor-trends-2023-02.

197 **comparing candidates to one another:** Taly Reich, Jennifer Savary, and Daniella Kupor, "Evolving Choice Sets: The Effect of Dynamic (vs. Static) Choice Sets on Preferences," *Organizational Behavior and Human Decision Processes* 164 (May 2021): 147–57, https://doi.org /10.1016/j.obhdp.2021.03.003.

198 **belief that prestigious companies:** Daniel B. Turban and Daniel M. Cable, "Firm Reputation and Applicant Pool Characteristics," *Journal of Organizational Behavior* 24, no. 6 (August 12, 2003): 733–51, https://doi.org/10.1002/job.215.

209 **how people transfer knowledge:** Donald R. Hillman, "Understanding Multigenerational Work-Value Conflict Resolution," *Journal of Workplace Behavioral Health* 29, no. 3 (2014): 240–57, https://doi.org /10.1080/15555240.2014.933961.

210 **absorptive capacity is the ability:** María Magdalena Jiménez-Barrionuevo, Víctor J. García-Morales, and Luis Miguel Molina, "Validation of an Instrument to Measure Absorptive Capacity," *Technovation* 31, no. 5–6 (2011): 190–202, https://doi.org/10.1016/j.technovation.2010 .12.002.

INDEX

absorptive capacity, 210
acronyms, 33–35, 39
age, 146, 147
Andersen, Erin, 48, 50
applying for jobs, xxxiv, 36, 162–63
   miscommunications and, 79–80
   tailoring materials to each job,
     40–41
   see also interviews; résumés
artificial intelligence (AI), 192

Baker, Tricia, 74–75, 221–25, 227
Barbieri, Joshua, 51–52
Bogran, Vannessa, 204–5
boomers, 210
Brassey, Jacqui, xii
buzzwords, 31–33

career goers, xiv–xvii, 19, 179–80
   emotions of, x–xiii, 15, 221–25
     guilt, 222–23
     mixed, 225–26
   quiz for, xxiii–xxv
   see also specific categories

Changes to My Job checklist, 63
Conaty, Meghan, 77, 85–87
conversations, frank, 226–28
cover letters, 36, 40–41, 82
COVID pandemic, 57–58, 133, 164
Crisis of Identity career goers,
   xv–xviii, 1–56, 75, 76, 91,
   93, 110, 115, 125, 180, 196
career identity and
   centrality of, 7–11, 13–15, 108
   clarity check-in for, 27–28
   Die Harders and, 11–13
   Get-Me-Outers and, 11–13
   Happy Distancers and, 11, 12
   interviews and, 41–43
   low, and readiness to leave, 15
   measuring multiple times,
     13–14
   new, clarity around, 19–21
   new, networking for building,
     19, 21–22
   organizational versus
     professional, 7
   satisfaction in, 7–11, 13–15, 108

Crisis of Identity (*cont.*)
　strength of, 6–14
　Thrivers and, 10–11
　defined, 4–6
　hidden curriculums and, 28–31,
　　45–46
　jargon and, 31–36, 39
　interview questions to ask,
　　45–54
　　on amount of direct
　　　experience necessary,
　　　51–52
　　on availability of hands-on
　　　training, 52–53
　　on reasons others have failed,
　　　53–54
　interviews and, 36, 41–54
　　career identity and, 41–43
　　career story and, 43–45
　networking and, 28, 29, 38
　　forming connections, 24–25
　　for identity building, 19,
　　　21–22
　　identity clarity check-in and,
　　　27–28
　　with people in
　　　nonoverlapping career
　　　groups, 23–24
　　what to ask, 25–26
　　who to network with,
　　　22–23
　quiz for, xxiii–xxv
　skills of, 28
　　"break it down and build it
　　　back up" approach to,
　　　37–40
　　keeper, 16–19, 26, 36
　　on résumé, 36–37

　stage one: why am I unhappy
　　here?, xxvi, 6–15, 36
　　take-homes for, 55
　stage two: what do I want my
　　future career to look like?,
　　xxvi–xxvii, 16–28, 36
　　take-homes for, 55
　stage three: go on a fact-finding
　　mission to test whether a
　　career is a good fit for you,
　　xxvi, xxvii, 28–36
　　take-homes for, 55
　stage four: landing the job you
　　will love, xxvi, xxvii, 36–54
　　take-homes for, 56

Daily Stress Test, xxvii–xxxii, 14,
　49, 167
Davachi, Lila, 105–6
day-to-day roles, 109, 114, 158, 159
dentists, 52
Denzer, Ben, 121
Die Harders, 11–13
disruptions, *see* interruptions
divorce, xiv–xv, 15
Dobrow, Shoshana, 19–20, 23, 42
Drifted Apart career goers,
　xv–xvi, xviii–xix, 57–88,
　91, 180
　and changes in the industry,
　　72–75
　and changes in the workplace,
　　60–67, 76
　　organizational-level, 61, 62,
　　　64–67
　and changes in yourself, 61,
　　67–71
　defined, 59–62

interviews and, 62
   skill evaluation in, 84–86
   storytelling in, 86–87
networking and, 61, 71–73,
   75–79
   identifying potential
      organizations first, 76–77
   keeping track of shared and
      unshared experiences,
      78–79
   reaching out to employees of
      those organizations, 77–78
preferences and, 69–71, 75–78
quiz for, xxiii–xxv
skills of
   framing to maximize fit,
      82–84
   interviews and, 84–86
stage one: why am I unhappy
   here?, xxvi, 62–71
   take-homes for, 87
stage two: what do I want my
   future career to look like?,
   xxvi–xxvii, 61, 71–79
   take-homes for, 88
stage three: go on a fact-finding
   mission to test whether a
   career is a good fit for you,
   xxvi, xxvii, 61, 79–82
   take-homes for, 88
stage four: landing the job you
   will love, xxvi, xxvii, 82–87
   take-homes for, 88
Dumitru, Oana, 208

emotions, x–xiii, 15, 221–25
   guilt, 222–23
   mixed, 225–26

employee resource group
   (ERG), 160
experience, 51–53, 127
   overselling, 37, 83–84, 172
   status and, 144, 147
   see also skills
expertise, 83, 144

failure, fear of, 15
feedback, 53, 128, 136, 137,
   139, 140
   following promotion failures or
      successes, 169

Galinsky, Adam, 39–40
gender, 144, 146, 169
generational differences,
   209–10
Get-Me-Outers, 11–13
Gonzalez, Victor M., 118
Gordon, Amie, xxvii
guilt, 222–23

Happy Distancers, 11, 12
health care industry, 13
Heasman, Dan, 85–86
hidden curriculums, 28–31,
   45–46, 72
Higgins, Monica, 19–20,
   23, 42
hot desking, 118, 119
hoteling, 57–58, 118
Hudson, Nathan, 67–68

IBM, 192
identities, 6–7
   career, 107, 125
      roles and, 108–10

identities (*cont.*)
  working spheres and, 128
  see also Crisis of Identity
    career goers
interruptions, 92–94, 101–4, 107,
    108, 128
  and ability to pick up where you
    left off, 104–7
  documenting, 106–7, 128
  external, 102, 103, 128
  internal, 102, 106, 108
  memory formation and, 105–6
  office layout and, 116–18
  self-, 104
  workspaces and, 118–19
interviews, xvi, 77, 79, 226–27
  Crisis of Identity career goers
    and, 36, 41–54
    career identity and, 41–43
    career story and, 43–45
  Drifted Apart career goers
    and, 62
    skill evaluation in, 84–86
    storytelling in, 86–87
  miscommunications in, 80
  Runner-Up career goers and
    hedging about preparation in,
      172–73
    and list of changes you might
      encounter, 164–67
    parallel or step-down moves
      and, 174–75
    promotion decision-makers
      and, 167–68
    researching the company
      beforehand, 173–74
  Stretched Too Thin career
    goers and

  juggling multiple roles and,
    127–28
  and which roles you would
    give up, 129–30
  Underappreciated Star career
    goers and, 195–96, 211–12
  underappreciation levels and,
    204–6
interviews, questions to ask in, xvi
  for Crisis of Identity career
    goers
    on amount of direct
      experience necessary,
      51–52
    on availability of hands-on
      training, 52–53
    on reasons others have failed,
      53–54
  critical, 81–82
    on goal of the interview,
      46–47
    on how the job came to be,
      47–48
    on interviewer's interface
      with hiring manager,
      48–49
    on interviewing at the
      office, 50
    on what the day-to-day of the
      job looks like, 49
  for Runner-Up career goers
    on feedback process, 169
    on protocol for sourcing and
      reviewing applicants,
      168–69
    on succession plan, 170–71
    on type of skills needed,
      169–70

investigative questions, 227–28
"I Was Absent That Day," 29–30

jargon, 36, 39, 83, 158, 208
  acronyms, 33–35, 39
  learning, 31–36
  likelihood of encountering,
    33–34
  when to use, 39–40
Jerks at Work (West), x, 53
jobs
  advertisements for, 28, 48, 49, 80
  creators of, 80–81, 164
  applying for, *see* applying
    for jobs
  titles of, 164
jolts, 142, 150–52, 169–70
JPMorgan Chase, 215

Kalpathi, Subbu, 153, 174–75, 193,
  206–7
Kilduff, Gavin, 148
knowledge transfer, 209–11

language
  in describing job issues, xii–xiii
  jargon, *see* jargon
Leach, Colin Wayne, 7
LinkedIn, xvi, xxxiii, 77, 200
  researching companies on,
    173, 174
  résumé and, 127

Mao, Ethan, 44–45, 49, 78, 83–84
Mark, Gloria, 110, 117, 118
McGovern, Michele, 32
McKinsey & Company, 72
McKinsey Health Institute, xii

memory formation, and
  interruptions, 105–6
Miles, John, 201–2, 215, 225–26
millennials, 209–10

nepotism, 146, 169
networking, xvi, xxxii–xxxiii
  for Crisis of Identity career
    goers, 28, 29, 38
  forming connections, 24–25
  for identity building, 19,
    21–22
  identity clarity check-in and,
    27–28
  with people in
    nonoverlapping career
    groups, 23–24
  what to ask, 25–26
  who to network with, 22–23
  daily goals for, 25
  for Drifted Apart career goers,
    61, 71–73, 75–79
  identifying potential
    organizations first, 76–77
  keeping track of shared and
    unshared experiences,
    78–79
  reaching out to employees of
    those organizations, 77–78
  information overlap in, 23, 78
  snowball sampling in, 24–25
  for Runner-Up career goers,
    156–60
  status and, 148–50
  for Stretched Too Thin career
    goers, 98
  questions to ask, 113–15
  role priorities and, 112–13

networking (*cont.*)
  Underappreciated Star career
    goers and, 186, 196, 199
networks
  broad, 24
  dense, 22, 23, 25
  identity-based, 24
  size versus quality of, 25
newcomer hump, 207–9
New York University, x
  hiring and promotions at,
    157–58, 168–69
no, saying, 123–24, 165
"nobody told me that" exercise,
    29–31, 45, 51, 72, 95,
    135, 203
norms, 28–31, 45–46, 72, 83,
    112, 115, 116, 122, 156–58,
    208, 227
NPR, 29–30

office environments, 50
  artifacts in, 118–20
  hot desking, 118, 119
  hoteling, 57–58, 118
  interruptions and, 116–18
  office layout, 116–18, 120–22
  remote work, 119–20, 147,
    150, 151
  roles and, 120–22, 129

passion roles, 109–10, 114–15, 129,
    158–60
Passion Struck (Miles), 202
Perel, Esther, 227–28
personality traits, 67
PhDs, 199–200
Power of Us, The (Van Bavel), 6

preferences, 69–71, 75–78, 188
Priddle, Charlotte, 120–24,
    127, 128
promotions, 135
  and accuracy of reading the
    status hierarchy, 148–50
  alternative paths to, 148–49
  denials of, 135–37, 142, 150
    boss's amount of influence
      and, 142, 148–49, 153, 168
    feedback process
      following, 169
    jolts and, 142, 150–52
    reasons for, 137–42, 160, 161,
      170–71
    structural roadblocks and,
      142, 153–56
  emergency, 133–34
  lack of knowledge about
    competition for, 162,
    168, 197
  missed middle steps in,
    134–35, 157
  as mixed bag, 165
  nepotism and, 146, 169
  reasons for, 137, 140–41, 146
  Runner-Up career goers and,
    156, 163
  and accuracy of reading
    the status hierarchy,
    148–50
  asking the right questions
    about opportunities for,
    156–57
  and competition for scarce
    roles, 161–63, 168
  and difference in
    responsibilities, 171–73

feedback process
following, 169
and filling in missed roles to
be competitive, 157–58
interviews and, 167–68
job titles and, 164
lack of knowledge about
competition for, 162, 168
list of changes you might
encounter after, 164–67
next-step jobs and, 142, 154
protocol for sourcing and
reviewing applicants for,
168–69
succession plans and, 170–71
skills and, 169–70
status and, 146, 150, 170
stress following, 165, 167
Underappreciated Star career
goers and, 186, 188, 196
psychological issues, x–xvii

questions, investigative,
227–28

race, 144, 146, 169
relationships, xiv–xv, 12, 13, 15,
59–61, 133, 219, 220, 224
with careers, x–xiii, xv, 219
conflicts in, 136–37, 141
miscommunications in, 80
time and energy for, 90, 93
remote workers, 119–20, 147,
150, 151
résumés, xvi, xxxiv, 18, 35, 36, 82,
162, 214
cover letters for, 36, 40–41, 82
framing of skills on, 36–37

jargon on, 34, 83
LinkedIn and, 127
overlapping employment dates
on, 125–27
overselling contributions on,
83–84
"safe," 42
risk-taking, 201–3, 206–7, 226
roles and responsibilities
career identity and, 108–10
day-to-day roles, 109, 114,
158, 159
diminishing returns on, 159
hidden barriers to, 163
passion roles, 109–10, 114–15,
129, 158–60
Stretched Too Thin career goers
and, 116, 125
giving up jobs to take on a
new role, 129–30
networking based on
priorities in, 112–13
office space and, 120–22, 129
overlap in, 113–14
overlapping employment
dates and, 125–27
prioritizing jobs and, 128
ranking from most to least
relevant, 108–10
and saying no, 123–24, 165
swan cultures and, 122–23
visibility and status of, 97–99,
143, 159, 160, 187
volunteer, 95–101, 143
taking on too many, 93–104,
107, 108, 165
because you're the only
logical choice, 98–100

roles and responsibilities (*cont.*)
  as free-rider correction,
    100–101
  Underappreciated Star career
    goers and, 194
  up-and-out roles, 109, 114,
    158–61
Runner-Up career goers, xv–xvi,
    xxi, 11, 132–77
  defined, 135–36
  feedback and, 136, 137, 139, 140
  interview questions to ask
    on feedback process, 169
    on protocol for sourcing and
      reviewing applicants,
      168–69
    on succession plan, 170–71
    on type of skills needed,
      169–70
  interviews and
    hedging about preparation in,
      172–73
    and list of changes you might
      encounter, 164–67
    parallel or step-down moves
      and, 174–75
    promotion decision-makers
      and, 167–68
    researching the company
      beforehand, 173–74
  networking and, 156–60
  promotion denials and, 135–37,
    142, 150
    boss's amount of influence
      and, 142, 148–49, 153, 168
    feedback process
      following, 169
    jolts and, 142, 150–52

reasons for, 137–42, 160, 161,
  170–71
structural roadblocks and,
  142, 153–56
promotions and, 156, 163
and accuracy of reading the
  status hierarchy, 148–50
asking the right questions
  about opportunities for,
  156–57
and competition for scarce
  roles, 161–63, 168
and difference in
  responsibilities, 171–73
feedback process
  following, 169
and filling in missed roles to
  be competitive, 157–58
interviews and, 167–68
job titles and, 164
lack of knowledge about
  competition for, 162, 168
list of changes you might
  encounter after, 164–67
next-step jobs and, 142, 154
protocol for sourcing and
  reviewing applicants for,
  168–69
succession plans and,
  170–71
quiz for, xxiii–xxv
stage one: why am I unhappy
  here?, xxvi, 136–56
  take-homes for, 176
stage two: what do I want my
  future career to look like?,
  xxvi–xxvii, 156–63
  take-homes for, 176

stage three: go on a fact-finding mission to test whether a career is a good fit for you, xxvi, xxvii, 163–71
take-homes for, 176–77
stage four: landing the job you will love, xxvi, xxvii, 171–75
take-homes for, 177
status and
accuracy in reading the hierarchy of, 148–50
knowing how much you have, 142–47, 159
up-and-out roles and, 158–61

Salesforce, 24
side jobs, 126
skills, 206
acknowledgment of, 189–91
of Crisis of Identity career goers, 28
"break it down and build it back up" approach to, 37–40
keeper, 16–19, 26, 36
on résumé, 36–37
diminishing returns problem with, 199
of Drifted Apart career goers framing to maximize fit, 82–84
interviews and, 84–86
expertise in, 83, 144
"good enough," 199–201
knowledge transfer and, 209–11
overselling, 37, 83–84, 172
promotions and, 169–70
status and, 144, 147

training in, 52–53, 170
of Underappreciated Star career goers
acknowledgment of, 191
and evaluating star status, 185–86
impact on performance, 183–85
rare, 184–86
rare, being better than others at, 185, 186
talking about, in relation to outcomes, 213–14
STAR method, 86
status, 143, 154
age and, 147
of boss, 153–54, 168
conferral process of, 147
cues to, 144–47, 149–50, 169
hierarchy of, 142, 146, 148–49
jolts and, 142, 150–52
interpersonal dynamics and, 146
job titles and, 164
networking and, 148–50
prestige-based, 144–47, 169, 180–81
promotions and, 146, 150, 170
Runner-Up career goers and
accuracy in reading the hierarchy of, 148–50
knowing how much you have, 142–47, 159
taking on roles to increase, 97–99, 143, 159, 160
Underappreciated Star career goers and, 180, 187–89, 191, 206–9
measuring, 181–86

STEM, 24
stressors
  identity and, 14
  promotions as, 165, 167
  self-interruptions triggered
    by, 104
  unanticipated, xxxi–xxxii
Stress Test, Daily, see Daily
  Stress Test
Stretched Too Thin career goers,
  xv–xvi, xix–xx, 89–131,
  165, 180
  defined, 92–93
  interruptions and, 92–94,
    101–4, 107, 108, 128
    and ability to pick up where
      you left off, 104–7
    documenting, 106–7, 128
    external, 102, 103, 128
    internal, 102, 106, 108
    memory formation and,
      105–6
    office layout and, 116–18
    self-, 104
    workspaces and,
      118–19
  interviews and
    juggling multiple roles and,
      127–28
    and which roles you would
      give up, 129–30
  networking and, 98
    questions to ask, 113–15
    role priorities and,
      112–13
  quiz for, xxiii–xxv
  roles and responsibilities and,
    116, 125

giving up jobs to take on a
    new role, 129–30
  networking based on
    priorities in, 112–13
  office space and, 120–22, 129
  overlap in, 113–14
  overlapping employment
    dates and, 125–27
  prioritizing jobs and, 128
  ranking from most to least
    relevant, 108–10
  and saying no, 123–24, 165
  swan cultures and,
    122–23
  three categories of roles,
    109–10, 114–15, 129
  visibility and status of, 97–99,
    143, 159, 160, 187
  volunteer, 95–101, 143
roles and responsibilities, taking
    on too many, 93–104, 107,
    108, 165
  because you're the only
    logical choice, 98–100
  as free-rider correction,
    100–101
stage one: why am I unhappy
    here?, xxvi, 93–108
  take-homes for, 130
stage two: what do I want my
    future career to look like?,
    xxvi–xxvii, 107–15
  take-homes for, 130
stage three: go on a fact-finding
    mission to test whether a
    career is a good fit for you,
    xxvi, xxvii, 115–24
  take-homes for, 130–31

stage four: landing the job you
will love, xxvi, xxvii,
125–30, 172
take-homes for, 131
working spheres and, 110–11,
114, 116–19, 128, 129
succession plans, 170–71
swan cultures, 122–23

task switching, 90, 92, 94, 111
Three Things Exercise, 17–18, 21,
26, 38, 40
Underappreciated Star career
goers and, 181–83, 191, 213
Thrivers, 10–11
Tincup, William, xxxiv, 49, 80–81
training, 52–53, 170
"tricky situations at work"
exercise, 99
20 Slices of American Cheese
(Denzer), 121

uncertainty, fear of, 225–26
Underappreciated Star career
goers, xv–xvi, xxii, 11, 171,
178–217
appreciation wish list for,
187–88, 212–13
company's Achilles' heel and,
215–16
competition and, 197–99
defined, 180–81
forms of underappreciation,
186–89
compensation, 186, 188, 193
networking, 186, 196, 199
promotion opportunities,
186, 188, 196

skill acknowledgment,
189–91
"good enough" skills and,
199–201
interviews and, 195–96, 211–12
underappreciation levels and,
204–6
knowledge transfer and, 209–11
levels of underappreciation, 192
company, 193
interpersonal relationships,
194–95
interviews and, 204–6
market, 192–93
role, 194
newcomer hump and,
207–9
quiz for, xxiii–xxv
risk-taking and, 201–3,
206–7
skills of
acknowledgment of, 191
and evaluating star status,
185–86
impact on performance,
183–85
rare, 184–86
rare, being better than others
at, 185, 186
talking about, in relation to
outcomes, 213–14
stage one: why am I unhappy
here?, xxvi, 189–96, 204
take-homes for, 216
stage two: what do I want my
future career to look like?,
xxvi–xxvii, 196–204
take-homes for, 217

Underappreciated Star (*cont.*)
  stage three: go on a fact-finding
    mission to test whether a
    career is a good fit for you,
    xxvi, xxvii, 203–11
  take-homes for, 217
  stage four: landing the job you
    will love, xxvi, xxvii,
    211–16
  take-homes for, 217
  status and, 180, 187–89, 191,
    206–9
  measuring, 181–86
  Three Things Exercise and,
    181–83, 191, 213

up-and-out roles, 109, 114,
  158–61
U.S. Bureau of Labor Statistics, 72

Vaisman, Sima, 41–42
Van Bavel, Jay J., 6–7, 13
Vidal Sassoon, 51–52

Wee, Elijah, 151
working spheres, 110–11, 114,
  116–19, 128, 129
work-life balance, 167
World Economic Forum, 94

Yu, Siyu, 148